Keep the Fires Burning

by Michael Lane

evidence4faith.org

Keep the Fires Burning
Copyright © 2024 Michael Lane

ISBN: 979-8-9909910-0-2

Evidence 4 Faith is a 501(c)(3) registered non-profit organization based in the United States of America. For more information on Evidence 4 Faith (E4F), visit evidence4faith.org on the web.

Cover design by Charlotte Fohner, composited with images by Nick Dunlap, Chirag Nayak, CHUTTERSNAP, Marek Piwnicki, Mulyadi, Paul Bulai, Ricardo Gomez Angel, Toa Heftiba, Tobias Rademacher, and Patrick Hendry on Unspalsh. Read about the Unsplash license at unsplash.com/license.

Dedication

I wish to dedicate this book to a mentor of mine, Dr. Dan Hayden. I was introduced to Dan back in the 1980s at Fort Wilderness Ministries where Dan once worked and where I would later serve. It was his teachings from the Word of God that made an impact on me. By listening intently to Dan teach, I studied his style, content, format, and delivery. The Holy Spirit used Dan to instruct me. His exposition and comprehensive explanation of Scripture not only captured my intellect, but through the Spirit, he taught me how to take a passage and verse and allow God to enter my mind and perform a metamorphosis, not only in my cognitive capacities, but in my life as well. I thank God for bringing Dan Hayden into my life and using him to even point me on the road to serving Christ Jesus full time. To this servant of God, I dedicate this book.

Special Thanks

I wish to say thank you to the people who helped us make this book a reality.

To Constance Hendricks, the wife of a member of Evidence 4 Faith's board of directors who served as an editor in producing this book.

I also want to thank my sister Bonnie Lane, a former missionary who also helped in editing the text and also in formatting the Fan the Flames discussion questions that appear at the end of each chapter.

Thank you to Charlotte Fohner who designed this book and helped it become a reality.

Table of Contents

Follow along with the podcast!
Scan the QR code or search
"Keep the Fires Burning" at
evidence4faith.org/courses.

Introduction

Those who grew up attending Sunday School, Christian programs like Awana or some other organization, probably grew up hearing a lot of Bible stories. Some of these are well-known and taught so frequently that many can quote the story themselves and give details about the characters in them. For instance, David and Goliath. Even non-Christians know this famous Bible story of a shepherd boy who slayed a huge dude with a sling. Others know of Moses and the crossing of the Red Sea and the Ten Commandments. Still, many can recall details and lessons they have heard from such famous characters as Abraham, Jacob, Samson, Peter, Paul, Solomon, Samuel, Joseph, Daniel, Joshua, etc. The list goes on. There are so many great individuals described in the Bible and the lessons we can learn from them has supplied ministers, pastors, and missionaries with sermons for centuries. And why not? These are easy to read and garnish. The Holy Spirit uses such key figures to teach us lessons that help us grow and stay in a close relationship with Jesus and the Father. As the apostle John so eloquently wrote 2,000 years ago...

I John 2:24 (GW)
Make sure that the message you heard from the beginning lives in you. If that message lives in you, you will also live in the Son and in the Father.

Even though there are over 3,200 individual characters named in the Bible, we tend to naturally focus on maybe 100 major characters. These are the ones we get to know well. Others are only named once and often in just a listing of genealogies or in a specific roll call. Some are not even named; their personal identity being expunged from human history. But there are many of what I am terming lesser-known characters that will be spotlighted in this study. In cases such as these, God has allowed us a bit more information about their lives. Why does He do this? No man can fully understand Almighty God, but it seems reasonable to me that one reason He gave us just a bit more information on certain people is to aid in our relationship with Him. After all, God is relational. He wants us to abide with Him. This word "abide" that is frequently used in John 15 is the Greek word **μένω meno** which is a verb and is often translated as dwell, remain, or continue. Thus, for us to abide with someone, we must first be with the person in some form of relationship. This is the root of our salvation through faith in Jesus Christ. We are adopted into God's family with the full rights of being His children.

One normal aspect of a family is passing down family stories and legends. Most people can probably recall sitting with a family member and listening to stories. My grandkids love to sit and listen to me tell stories about my life when I was younger and of the adventures I experienced. I can recall this past winter when I sat with my granddaughter Cora by my fireplace and told her of some of my adventures. I then related a lesson that would help her in growing up and living a life for God. By hearing of my faults along with my successes, I hope that she will glean something from those stories and adventures that will benefit her life and help her.

That is the purpose of this book, for us to abide closer to Christ by listening to some of the lesser-known characters found in His 66 love letters He has bestowed to us. My hope and prayer are that some of these lessons will draw you deeper into a close relationship with Jesus that will, even in your golden years, keep your fire burning hot for Him.

Boaz

A Godly Gentleman

A teacher friend of mine once told me of a situation that happened to him. He was working in his room after school, and it was getting quite late. He thought he was the only person still in the building, but he wasn't. As he worked in his room, suddenly, in came one of his high school students. She was one of the prettiest girls in the school and had frequently been one of his students. He was pleasantly surprised to see her walk in and asked her why she was still in the building. She made some reply, but it didn't seem to register because she then closed the door behind her and walked over to where he was sitting. He thought, "What is going on here?"

She sat down across from him. Her smile lit up her face as she said, "I am glad you are still here. I was afraid that you had left." He asked her again why she was there, and she told him what was on her mind. She unbuttoned the top button on her blouse as she told him that she wanted to have an affair with him. That it would be just their secret. No one was in the building and so no one would know. They could meet like this as often as he wanted. She said that she knew he would never divorce his wife, and that was okay. She wanted to just have this time with him until she left for college. No commitments and no hang-ups.

We know about Boaz from the Book of Ruth. But how often do we study about this man who was not only an ancestor of King

David, but also of Jesus, the Messiah? Let's take a look at an extremely valuable lesson this man can teach us.

Boaz doesn't come into the picture of Ruth until chapter 2.

Ruth 2:1 (ESV)
Now Naomi had a relative of her husband's, a worthy
man of the clan of Elimelech, whose name was Boaz.

From this sentence we find that he was indeed a relative of Naomi's late husband, Elimelech. He was most likely a cousin of Elimelech, but we are not certain as the Bible is silent on the specifics of this relationship. In any case, Boaz was described as **"worthy"** which in the Hebrew is לַיִח pronounced **chayil**, which means he had power and/or wealth. It is interesting to note that this is the exact same Hebrew word used to describe the Queen of Sheba who once visited Solomon (I Kings 10:2; II Chronicles 9:1). Boaz also owned many fields around the Bethlehem region, which was where this story took place. These same fields are the sites of many famous events in biblical history, such as where David watched the family sheep, where the Christmas story occurs, where Joseph and the shepherds were, and also the site of Rachel's tomb, which would have been present and visible in the days of Boaz.

The next mention of Boaz shows us something of his faith and relationship with God.

Ruth 2:4 (ESV)
And behold, Boaz came from Bethlehem. And he
said to the reapers, "The LORD be with you!"

This type of greeting gives us some indication that Boaz was walking with God. Despite the land having gone through a famine (Ruth 1:1) and was now being blessed again by the hand of God (Ruth 1:6), Boaz seems like one of those faithful followers of God who would remain close to God no matter the circumstances.

Genealogies listed at the end of the book of Ruth indicate that this is taking place during the later time of the period known as the Judges. The later Judges were men like Japheth, Samson, and Eli the High Priest. It was at a time when there was no king and the people would follow God only when a good Judge was leading them.

Boaz seemed to be a true Israelite. He was wealthy, powerful, well thought of, but single. There is no suggestion anywhere in the book that he was married. This seems to be rather odd given this culture at this time. The powerful and wealthy men who were walking with God and not involved in sinful behaviors were the ones that seemed to be very popular. He also seems to be much older than Ruth. Because later in the story he said to Ruth...

Ruth 3:10 (ESV)
"May you be blessed by the Lord, my daughter. You have made this last kindness greater than the first in that you have not gone after young men, whether poor or rich.

So why does it appear that Boaz is single? I believe that there must be a reason. He seems to be a caring individual with money and means. But to be as old as he must be and still be single seems odd for this culture. He appeared to have accepted this, for we don't see him chasing after Ruth or some other women. So, I suggest that he may have been a bit repulsive in appearance. I mean, let's be frank here. There seems to be something wrong with him since he has gone all of these years and is not married.

Now don't get me wrong. I am not saying that all men must be married. No way! I believe that marriage is a gift. Some men just don't have that gift! And this goes the same for women. Take note of the number of divorces there are in the country. I believe that some people are not meant to be married. I know both men and women who do not possess the gift of marriage.

Boaz was not married, but he was not dead either. When Ruth came by, she caught his eye.

Ruth 2:5 (ESV)
Then Boaz said to his young man who was in charge of the reapers, "Whose young woman is this?"

This verse also tells us something about Ruth. There were many other women in the fields (vs. 8) but Ruth stood out in a crowd. Men noticed her when she went by. She certainly caught Boaz's eye even though she was in a group of other women. So, he inquired about her. When he discovered that she was married to a relative of his, he treated her like family.

Ruth 2:8-9 (ESV)
Then Boaz said to Ruth, "Now, listen, my daughter, do not go to glean in another field or leave this one, but keep close to my young women. Let your eyes be on the field that they are reaping, and go after them. Have I not charged the young men not to touch you? And when you are thirsty, go to the vessels and drink what the young men have drawn."

He treated her this way because he knew the family history. But note that he did nothing about trying to pursue her as a wife, even though he knew the Law regarding this. Boaz seemed quite interested in her but didn't make a move to build a marriage with her. He, instead, treated her with familal respect. Then at lunchtime, Boaz gave her a meal.

Ruth 2:14 (ESV)
And at mealtime Boaz said to her, "Come here and eat some bread and dip your morsel in the wine." So she sat beside the reapers, and he passed to her roasted grain. And she ate until she was satisfied, and she had some left over.

After the meal, he gave the other men in the area strict commands not to bother her or pursue her, but to treat her like a family member of his.

Ruth 2:15-16 (ESV)
When she rose to glean, Boaz instructed his young men, saying, "Let her glean even among the sheaves, and do not reproach her. And also pull out some from the bundles for her and leave it for her to glean, and do not rebuke her."

I cannot help but think that the young men working for Boaz must have winked to each other knowing their boss was more than interested in this foreigner. Guys often do things like that. Notice, too, that he was providing for her in an ingenious way. And he told her that she could work in his fields until the harvest was over. That could be a couple of months (barley + wheat harvest).

Ruth 2:21 (ESV)
And Ruth the Moabite said, "Besides, he said
to me, 'You shall keep close by my young men
until they have finished all my harvest.'"

The story takes a turn where we find Ruth getting ready to propose to Boaz. (I told you he was slow at relationships.) But notice how Boaz handled this. First, Ruth cleansed herself and made sure she was smelling nice.

Ruth 3:3 (ESV)
Wash therefore and anoint yourself, and put on your cloak
and go down to the threshing floor, but do not make yourself
known to the man until he has finished eating and drinking.

She went to him in the middle of the night to a secluded place where he was sleeping and proposed marriage to him through her actions.

Ruth 3:7-8 (ESV)
And when Boaz had eaten and drunk, and his heart
was merry, he went to lie down at the end of the heap
of grain. Then she came softly and uncovered his feet
and lay down. At midnight the man was startled and
turned over, and behold, a woman lay at his feet!

She waited until Boaz had eaten and was full, celebrated with his wine, and went to sleep before making her move.

This passage sounds quite strange to us in our culture today, but in ancient Israel, this could mean two different things. The one is the literal approach that she just uncovers his feet. But in ancient Palestine this phrase also had a different meaning. It carried a sexual overtone. This phrase is used to mean genitals and is a way of referring to fondling. Now being from Moab,

Ruth would behave this way in a non-marriage relationship. But notice Boaz's reaction. The Hebrew word here is דָּרַד **charad**, which means he panicked. To be awaken from his wine-induced sleep in the middle of the night, smelling the perfume, and finding the presence of a woman next to him would scare this older bachelor to death.

I love Boaz's reaction. He was afraid, but his walk with God was so strong that he wanted to stop this. Unlike David who faltered greatly in a similar situation, Boaz handled this with great wisdom and self-control. He knew that this was a wedding proposal because she says to him...

Ruth 3:9 (ESV)
"I am Ruth, your servant. Spread your wings
over your servant, for you are a redeemer."

Boaz, who hadn't had a girl all of his life, was hit with the phrase, *Spread your wings over your servant*, which meant marriage.

He begins talking about how happy he would be to marry her and to do things right but not the way she was proposing. He told her that he would marry her, but that he would follow God's Law in this matter. He even then dismissed her before light to protect her reputation!

Ruth 3:14 (ESV)
So she lay at his feet until the morning, but arose before
one could recognize another. And he said, "Let it not be
known that the woman came to the threshing floor."

Though she stayed with him all night, there was no more activity. He most likely had her stay for protection, after all, there was a party that night with wine flowing generously. But he sent her away in the morning.

As the story goes on, we find Boaz fulfilling his vow to Ruth by going through the proper channels of God's Law. God blesses them also with children and the right to be included in the ancestry of Jesus.

Before leaving this, let's just quickly reexamine what happened that night at the threshing floor when Boaz was awakened by this young foreign woman who appeared to be quite attractive.

1. He stopped her.
2. Though she was there, a beautiful sight and willing, he would not take advantage of her.
3. He protected her reputation (more than she did).
4. Though tempted, he would not yield to his desires outside of marriage.

Boaz was patient. He waited for God to fulfill his wishes for a wife and when the opportunity came, he was a godly gentleman. We, too, need to be following the actions of Boaz and Joseph and not the example of David (2 Samuel 11).

The teacher at the beginning of this story was in a serious situation. He had a beautiful young lady sitting across from him who desired to have a more than platonic relationship with him. The building was indeed empty except for the two of them. She had plainly stated what she wanted from him, and she had even proceeded with the details of all that they could be doing together. It was a defining moment in this teacher's life.

When the student had finished her offer, he quietly arose and walked around the desk. He pulled back her chair and as she stood up, he backed away and said that she needed to leave right now. He told her that the promise he made to his wife was something that he was not going to break. He then escorted her out the door of his room telling her that she had the wrong idea about him. He told her that he was tempted, but that he would not break his word. She smiled and said, "Your loss." Then she left.

Fan the Flame

Have you ever wanted to "do the right thing" but temptation got the better of you? Why do you think that happened?

_____

_____

_____

_____

_____

The Bible has much to say about sexual sin including adultery (married people choosing sex with someone other than their spouse), and fornication (sex between single people). What are your beliefs?

_____

_____

_____

_____

_____

Look up these few references to see what God has to say about it. I've only included a few because of lack of space. However, you can further research this "hot" topic on your own. Exodus 20:14, Galatians 5:19-22, I Thessalonians 4:1-8 are just a few. Jot down what they say and take time to consider them carefully.

_____

_____

_____

Bartimaeus
A Behind-the-Scenes Man

Matthew 20:29-34; Mark 10:46-52; Luke 18:35-43

Those around her know my wife Denise as the "Queen of Treats." She got this title many years ago by making treats for youth groups at the church where I taught the senior high. But she didn't stop there. She made treats for the Bible club I sponsored at the public high school where I taught. She also made treats for the *In Pursuit* college program at a Christian camp I worked at for years. She continues to make treats for Bible studies, staff meetings, and just about any other event or "excuse" she can find.

What do I mean by treats? Well, I am not just speaking of one type of cookie, she makes the most delicious chocolate chip cookies and many other varieties. She makes chocolate éclair cake, brownies with many variations, bricklebars, chocolate mayonnaise cake, frosted chocolate chewies, cheesecake, ice-cream cakes, and a couple of dozen other exquisite, scrumptious delectable delicacies.

Yes, my wife is at home in the kitchen. She is most comfortable when she's behind the scenes. She does not like to be in the spotlight and is easily embarrassed by me when I praise her in front of others. However, she considers her ministry serious business, and she devotes many hours to it. She feels God has called her to be the treat maker for events.

Now, she will never be famous or well known to most people through her ministry, but she does impact people. In fact, though people know that she makes treats for events, some do not even know what she looks like. But they are often thankful for her ministry. I hear the praise often, and she does not. Some people can't handle that type of ministry. They need to hear the applause for their accomplishments. Not my wife. I bring home empty containers and that is her reward. She is content to know that her work is appreciated, though seldom does anyone ever see her actually working in her ministry.

Let's examine the life of a man few people can even recall from the Bible. His name is Bartimaeus, and this is his story, given to us to learn something about serving God.

Mark 10:46-52 (ESV)
And they came to Jericho. And as he was leaving Jericho with his disciples and a great crowd, Bartimaeus, a blind beggar, the son of Timaeus, was sitting by the roadside. And when he heard that it was Jesus of Nazareth, he began to cry out and say, "Jesus, Son of David, have mercy on me!" And many rebuked him, telling him to be silent. But he cried out all the more, "Son of David, have mercy on me!" And Jesus stopped and said, "Call him." And they called the blind man, saying to him, "Take heart. Get up; he is calling you." And throwing off his cloak, he sprang up and came to Jesus. And Jesus said to him, "What do you want me to do for you?" And the blind man said to him, "Rabbi, let me recover my sight." And Jesus said to him, "Go your way; your faith has made you well." And immediately he recovered his sight and followed him on the way.

This familiar passage is found in the three synoptic gospels, but it is only in Mark's Gospel that we find a name – Bartimaeus.

To begin, let's examine where and what is happening at this time

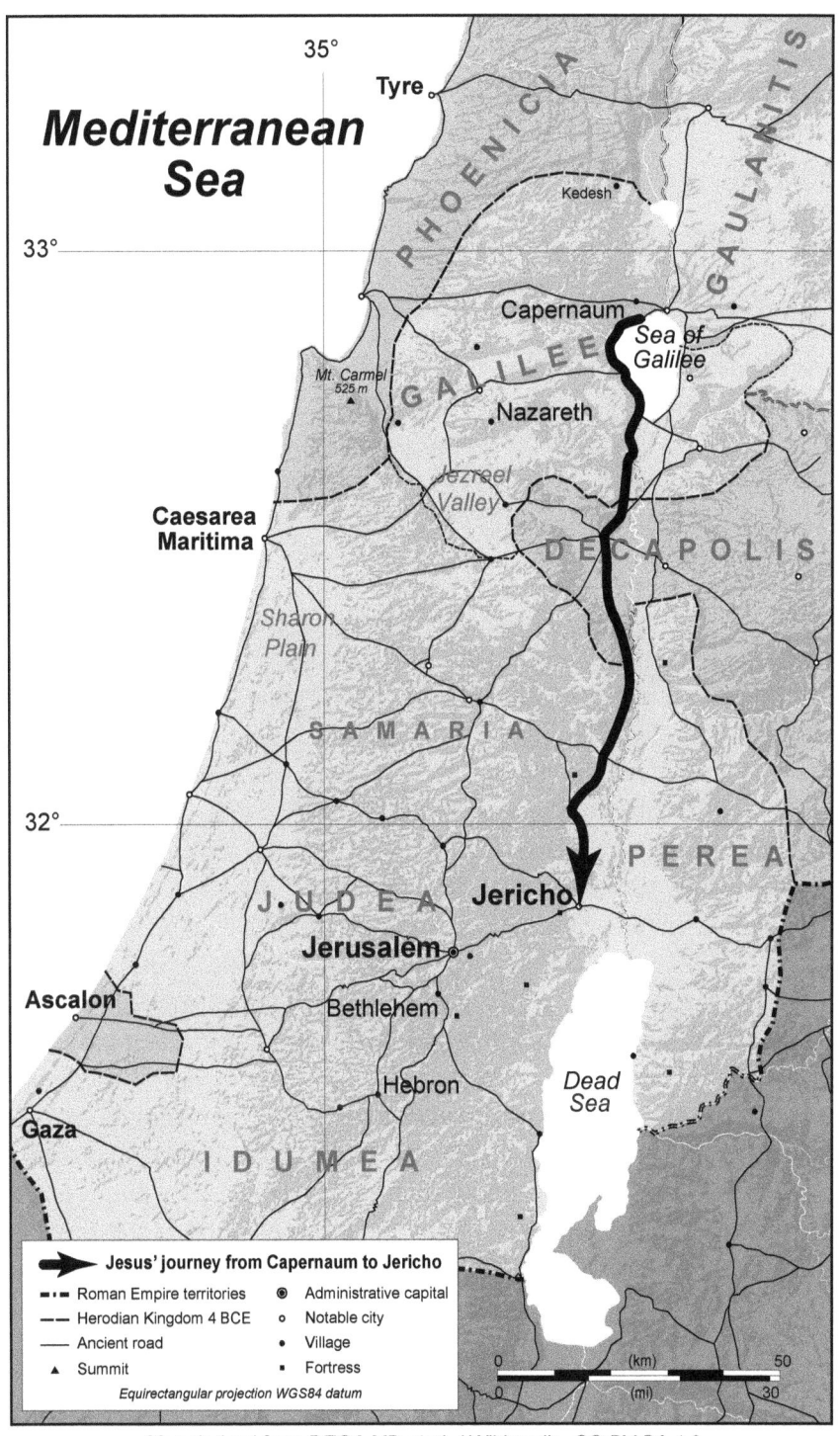

Mediterranean Sea

35°

Tyre

PHOENICIA

GAULANITIS

Kedesh

33°

Capernaum

Sea of Galilee

Mt. Carmel
525 m

GALILEE

Nazareth

Jezreel Valley

Caesarea Maritima

DECAPOLIS

Sharon Plain

SAMARIA

32°

PEREA

JUDEA

Jericho

Jerusalem

Ascalon

Bethlehem

Dead Sea

Hebron

Gaza

IDUMEA

Jesus' journey from Capernaum to Jericho

—·—· Roman Empire territories   ◉ Administrative capital
— — Herodian Kingdom 4 BCE   ○ Notable city
——— Ancient road   • Village
▲ Summit   ▪ Fortress

Equirectangular projection WGS84 datum

0   (km)   50
0   (mi)   30

13

in Jesus' life. He was on his final journey to Jerusalem from Galilee through Perea on the western side of the Jordan River. Jericho lies on this road, the turning point to Jerusalem. From Jericho the road meanders 15 miles to Jerusalem. It's while passing through Jericho that Jesus encountered our character.

Bartimaeus was one of the two blind men sitting at the road. We are not informed of the identity of the other blind man, but we are given Bartimaeus' name as one of the individuals.

As we examine Bartimaeus, we will notice a few details of his life from this passage, but most of his life is a mystery to us. In fact, if it were not for Mark's Gospel, we would not even know his name. But Mark does give us his name. As recorded, he is the son *(Bar)* of Timaeus. But what is given if we dig into these passages on this blind man?

First, as stated, he was blind. We do not know if Bartimaeus was blind from birth or if he lost his sight later in his life, but he had time to meet up with another blind man and together they staked themselves out in an excellent spot on a busy road. During the first century, people who were blind were often beggars and would commonly sit on popular roads and junctions near city gates. This was to beg for alms (charitable gifts). Almsgiving is not mentioned in the Old Testament, but according to the Law, Jews were to help other Jews avoid poverty (read Leviticus 25:35-38 and the example of Ruth and Boaz). But almsgiving became something more during the intertestamental times. Almsgiving became a command to show loving kindness, personal merit, and security. In Sirach 3:30 is recorded "almsgiving atones for sin" and in Tobit 4:10 is written that almsgiving "deliver[s] from death." Also in Tobit 12:8-9 it is written that almsgiving, along with prayer and fasting, is showing the highest expressions of Jewish piety. So that was the culture of the days of Jesus and where we find Bartimaeus. Bartimaeus thought God had made him blind, requiring him to beg Jews for alms so that the other people would obtain forgiveness for their sins. God never said this was true. This was a man-made tradition and not something from God.

Second, since he was blind and not capable of travel, I am curious as to how Bartimaeus heard about Jesus. Scholars are not sure that Jesus ever visited Jericho outside of this time in his ministry. So how did Bartimaeus know about Jesus? And how did he know that Jesus was the *Son of David*? Calling someone the *Son of David* was not just a reference of his genealogy, it was a Messianic title foretold in Psalm 89:3-4; Psalm 132:11-12; Isaiah 11:1-16; Isaiah 16:5; Jeremiah 23:5-6; Jeremiah 30:9; Ezekiel 37:24-28; Hosea 3:5; Zechariah 12:10.

Since Bartimaeus was unable to travel with Jesus and listen to his teaching prior to his Jericho experience, he must have listened carefully to what was being said about Jesus. No doubt Jesus was the hot topic of the day, but Bartimaeus seemed to have more knowledge of him than most others. He knows Jesus was a direct descendant of King David.

I find this point amazing. Bartimaeus never saw Jesus but had faith in him, not just as a healer, but as the Messiah and Son of God. Bartimaeus was not from Missouri, the "show me state." He believed without ever seeing him or even seeing Jesus perform miracles. This is tremendous faith! It was a faith that was not dependent upon tangibles but true faith and a strong belief. But where did this come from? How did Bartimaeus obtain this faith in the first century town of Jericho where Jesus had not yet even visited? The answer is obvious – someone had to tell him. Some unknown person or persons had spread the word about Jesus. I have often wondered who was responsible for telling Bartimaeus about Jesus. That message caused him to believe Jesus was Messiah as well as instilled faith that Jesus would indeed heal him.

This reminds me of another story. There was a boy who was born into a poor family in Massachusetts. He was one of nine children. When he was just four years old, his father died leaving the family in a bitter financial situation. With little schooling, he left his family at seventeen to work in his uncle's shoe shop in Boston. There in that shoe shop, he met Jesus as his Lord and Savior by the work of a humble man named Edward Kimble. That event changed this young man's life and the lives of millions of others all over the world. That young boy was none other than Dwight L. Moody. You have probably all heard of D.L. Moody, the famous evangelist of the 1800s, but how many of you recognized the name of Edward Kimble? Without Edward Kimble, there might not have been a D.L. Moody. I think that Bartimaeus had an Edward Kimble.

Third, "and immediately he recovered his sight and followed him on the way." Bartimaeus became a follower of Jesus, his Messiah. What happened to him after this moment in time is forever lost in the faded pages of history. Some believe that this silence was because he turned away from God during the Passion Week, thus his story does not have a good ending, as his faith dwindled, but I don't think that is the case. I believe that Bartimaeus might have been a background minister to God. I cite these reasons for this hypothesis.

First, he is mentioned by name and so is his father in Mark's Gospel. This makes it possible for readers of the text to go back and check the story to see if it is indeed true. The Gospel of Mark is thought to have been written between 40-61 A.D. It was one of the first Gospels written and circulated in the Roman Empire. Thus, many of the characters were still living after it was published. I believe that Mark might have written the names of these witnesses to the miracle because he wanted to make sure people could check his story to see that he was recording the truth.

Second, just because Bartimaeus is not mentioned during or after the Passion Week is not an indication that he turned away from Jesus. Maybe he had a family of his own. After he was miraculously healed maybe he went back home to his wife, kids, brothers, friends, to show them what Jesus had done for him. We don't know, but it seems logical. After all, when Jesus healed him, He commanded him in verse 52 to "go your way".

Third, recall that many people were following Jesus and their identities have been lost in time. Jesus had many men, women, and children accompanying him as he traveled. And we know that after Jesus returned to Heaven from the Mount of Olives, He had quite a large following of 120 (Acts 1:15). Could it be that Bartimaeus was present there in Jerusalem when Matthias was chosen? Could he have been present at Pentecost? We don't know. Scripture is silent on his life, but that doesn't mean that he deserted Jesus and his faith. He could have been a background Christian working for the Lord who dramatically changed his life.

Think about this; isn't it possible and logical that Bartimaeus would keep following Him after the spectacular way Jesus proved Himself as God to him? We know that then and even today there are many Christians that God uses in ministry who work in the background. Not all of God's faithful workers and servants are in the spotlight on the stage.

Our faith lesson here is based upon this idea. Bartimaeus was probably one of those Christians that God radically changed and who was quite happy serving God offstage. Too often we seem to think that to be in God's service requires us to be standing center stage with a vast crowd watching us. We think that to be in His service requires us to make a name for ourselves and be the major leader of a group. This is wrong theology. The Holy Spirit does not give everyone the gift of leadership. God needs followers and people willing to be offstage more than He needs leaders in the spotlight. For if everyone was in the spotlight, who would be doing all of the various other details?

Have you ever watched a modern motion picture and stayed around for the credits? I recently saw Prince Caspian at the theater. This movie, like many others, has a handful of major characters in it. After it was over, I sat and watched the credits and saw the *thousands* of people who worked to make this movie a success. It was not just the five main characters. Listed were people responsible for makeup, animation, special effects, grips, wranglers, caterers, and many more. It took a lot of people to make that one film a success. This is true of any major movie. Why do people think that if you are a Christian in God's service, you must be a leader and extremely visible?

In his book, *Beneath the Surface*, Bob Reccord writes about service for God. As he puts it, "It simply refers to the opportunity for God to use your life and mine in a special way to accomplish eternal things that will make an eternal difference in ourselves and others."

What kind of servant of Jesus are you? Are you called to be a stagehand for Him? If so, that is great! Are you called to be out in the open, loud, and visible for Him? If so, that is great, too. One is not more important than the others. As God tells us in I Corinthians 12, we are all part of the body of Christ. The Holy Spirit puts special gifts into each Christian for His service. Our job is to utilize them for His service to make eternal differences in people and us.

Louis Pasteur was not only one of the most brilliant scientists who ever lived, but he was also a man of compassion and of God. He believed strongly in the Bible and God blessed him tremendously, giving him insight into the field of immunology that was far beyond his peers. In fact, Pasteur was often ridiculed by his peers. Not just for his faith, but also for his ideas of how diseases are spread.

One project Pasteur worked on diligently was a vaccine for rabies. At that time in the 1800s, rabies killed thousands of people each year. Just as he developed his vaccine and was about to test it on himself, a nine-year-old boy was brought to him who had just been bitten by a rabid dog. Joseph Meister was the boy and his mother begged Pasteur to experiment on her son. Pasteur injected Joseph for ten days and he lived.

Decades later, when Louis Pasteur was nearing his death, he was asked what he wanted etched on his tombstone. Of all of his discoveries and services he had done for mankind, he asked that just three words be etched: Joseph Meister Lived.

The greatest legacy we can have as Christians is the people who live eternally with God because of our efforts and what He does in our lives.

Fan the Flame

God equips each of His children with gifts or talents with the intent that we use them to assist in building up each other and the Kingdom of God. Take a look at the following sources from the New Testament and list the gifts you see (Romans 12:6-8; I Corinthians 12:7-10; I Corinthians 12:28; Ephesians 4:11). Then take a close look at them to see which appear to have been given to you and make some notes on how you can use those gifts.

Jude
He Did What God Wanted, Not What He Wanted

Chuck Swindoll tells a story of when he had to fulfill an obligation to the U.S. Marine Corp. It happened just a few years after he and his wife, Cynthia, were married. He thought he was to serve in San Francisco, but he was ordered to report to Okinawa and leave Cynthia behind for 16 months. He speaks of how the both of them wept that night. They both felt upset that his orders were changed, and he would be gone for so long, so early in their marriage.

As he left, his brother handed him a book called *Through the Gates of Splendor.* It is a classic book about the five missionaries killed by the Auca Indians in Ecuador. Then when he landed in Okinawa, he eventually met a missionary named Bob Newkirk, who gave Chuck an Amplified Bible. Bob had marked one verse in that Bible, Philippians 3:10, and Chuck read it. He also spent many days in the home of that missionary.

For the first time in his life, Chuck was learning a new way of life. He found a new love for Christ that began to bloom on that island far away from home. Even though he didn't want to go, he had to, and it changed his life. Chuck Swindoll began his Christian work on that trip he didn't want to make.[1]

---

1 • As heard on Chuck Swindoll's *Insights for Living* Radio Show

Sometimes, we make plans or have intentions that just don't align with God's plan. Our plan might seem to make perfect sense to us and that it will yield great results, but God's plan is always better for His glory and purpose. In the opening story, Chuck Swindoll had what appeared to be a good plan with good intentions, but God did not allow him to carry through with it. It wasn't God's plan for his life. In this lesson, we will learn that Jude also experienced God changing his plan because, though it was a good plan, it wasn't in alignment with God's better plan.

Who was Jude? Nearly all scholars and early Church Fathers believed this Jude to be one of the half-brothers of Jesus. We get this idea from the first verse:

Jude 1:1 (ESV)
Jude, a servant of Jesus Christ and brother of James...

Yes, Jesus did have brothers, though they were half brothers because His father was God Himself. Matthew and Mark record part of Jesus' family:

Mark 6:3 (ESV)
Is not this the carpenter, the son of Mary and brother of James and Joses and Judas and Simon? And are not his sisters here with us?" And they took offense at him.

Jude is the Greek name for Judas or Jehudah, which means "praise of the Lord." It is one of those books of the Bible that most people seem to neglect. It is so small, only 25 verses, and tucked away in the back of the Bible so most people just don't pay much attention to it. Try to recall the last sermon you ever heard based upon the book of Jude. However, this little book is so important in our culture today. It would seem that Jude was alive here on earth and giving us a message straight from God that deals exactly with our culture today. It is hard to imagine that this was written 2,000 years ago.

Jude tells us right off why he wrote this. Of course, he was under the influence of the Holy Spirit, and this was not his undertaking (II Timothy 3:16). In his second sentence he gives us the purpose and reason for this book.

Jude 1:3 (ESV)

Beloved, although I was very eager to write to you about our common salvation, I found it necessary to write appealing to you to contend for the faith that was once for all delivered to the saints.

Now many people might just skim over this sentence without giving it much thought, but there is an important lesson here for us Christians. Jude wanted to write about salvation. It was on his heart, and he was eager to write about it. He even uses the term "eager" to describe how he felt. The word "eager" in the Greek language is **σπουδή spoude**, which also means diligence. However, he chose to follow the Spirit's lead and instead wrote this short essay about a serious problem. The Gnostics were perverting the grace of God. They were telling people that because Christ had forgiven them, they were free to sin as they wanted because their sins now would not be held against them.

Jude 1:4 (ESV)

For certain people have crept in unnoticed who long ago were designated for this condemnation, ungodly people, who pervert the grace of our God into sensuality and deny our only Master and Lord, Jesus Christ.

Jude 1:7 (ESV)

Just as Sodom and Gomorrah and the surrounding cities, which likewise indulged in sexual immorality and pursued unnatural desire, serve as an example by undergoing a punishment of eternal fire.

Jude is calling black, black, and white, white. He is not worried about being politically correct in his society. He is stating that this behavior is contrary to a Holy God and that He will punish people for this.

Sounds familiar to our society today, doesn't it? Several polls published show a remarkable trend of Christian thinking in this country. In these polls, over 67% state that homosexuality is not immoral. One poll taken of Christians now suggests that 62% of people say that sex between an unmarried man and woman is acceptable and 54% say that having a baby outside of marriage is acceptable. And these are so-called "Christian" poll results! As I researched and read many blogs and polls, I have found many people proclaiming that they are born-again Christians stating that God is a god of love and if two people love each other they can do what they want. God wants us to be happy because He loves us.

Jude was not the only Christian facing this type of worldview. The world that he lived in, with its Greek immorality and sensuality, had the same arguments we see today. As the saying goes, "There is nothing new under the sun."

Jude didn't want to write about this topic that was so controversial even in the Church back then. He wanted to write about the happy and joyful experience of salvation. But I am glad that He surrendered to the Holy Spirit's leadership. He concludes by giving us a warning that sounds as strong today as it must have been back then in the first century.

Jude 1:17-19 (ESV)
But you must remember, beloved, the predictions of the apostles of our Lord Jesus Christ. They said to you, "In the last time there will be scoffers, following their own ungodly passions." It is these who cause divisions, worldly people, devoid of the Spirit.

I do admire this man! This view was no doubt as unpopular with the public then as it is today! But he leaves us with a challenge that we all need to follow.

Jude 1:20-23 (ESV)
But you, beloved, building yourselves up in your most holy faith and praying in the Holy Spirit, keep yourselves in the love of God, waiting for the mercy of our Lord Jesus Christ that leads to eternal life. And have mercy on those who doubt; save others by snatching them out of the fire; to others show mercy with fear, hating even the garment stained by the flesh.

So, what is our faith lesson from Jude? It is simple. The time will come when you will remain quiet on a subject or talk about something that is politically correct so that no one is offended by what you say. Jude could have done that. He could have written a wonderful letter on salvation. But the Holy Spirit urged him to write on something that was going to be unpopular with many people, but it needed to be said. He chose to follow God's leading and not his own. We, too, should always follow God's leading, wherever it takes us.

Jenny sat in my lecture room, writing in her lab journal the protocol she had just followed. It was a time when the students often spoke on hot topics and whatever was on their minds.

Someone in the room asked me about the youth group I led in town, to which I answered. Then Jenny commented, "You know I go to church and attend a youth group." I told her that I already knew that. But then she said to me, "I would never go to your youth group or your church." When I asked her why, she said, "Because you are so judgmental on people. I really don't like that about you." I was puzzled and asked her to go on. She said that she had heard that I said that homosexuality and premarital sex were sins. She continued to say that I had no right to say such things were sins. After all, how did I know that they were sins today?

I waited a moment to see how the rest of the class was responding to this attack and I was amazed at how many students were sitting there with their mouths open, staring at me. I responded by saying that I believe that lying is a sin. I believe that stealing is a sin, no matter what you steal. I believe that cursing using God's name is a sin. I believe that murder is a sin, even to the point of planning the murder, not just carrying it out. I said that I believe that even looking at someone and thinking sexual fantasies about that person was a sin. Then I paused before continuing to let that sink in and to see how Jenny was responding. No comments were made by anyone. Then I said that it is true that I believe homosexuality is a sin as is premarital sex. But then I told my class, "I am not the one who made up those laws. God is the one who says them and because He says them, I believe Him!" Then I said, "I can see why someone would call me judgmental, but to be honest, I, too, have sinned and need God to forgive me and help me not to sin again. I don't justify my sins. Instead, I pray to God to help me not to do them again. That is what Jesus taught. It is called repentance, to change the direction in your life. This was Jesus' message to sinners. Repent and turn to God for salvation." Then I quoted a verse in I Peter:

1 Peter 1:16 (ESV)
Since it is written, "You shall be holy, for I am holy."

I told Jenny that if I seem judgmental to her, it is because I am quoting a God who is the Judge and knows what is right and wrong. I am not judging people, because I make mistakes too. But there is a difference. When I know I sin, I try everything to not do that sin again. I don't keep on doing it, flaunting God's commands. Some people try to justify their sins or say that they are not sinning or that society says it's okay. But I choose God over society. Society can say whatever it wants and constantly keeps changing with cultures. But that doesn't make it right. What God says is right and what I believe is true. His laws are based upon His character, not what changing cultures say.

Fan the Flame

As Christians, we know that Christ forgives our sins when we confess them (I John 1:9). Do you believe that you are free to sin any time you want? If so, why?

What does Paul say about continuing to sin in Romans 6:1-2, 12-13; I Thessalonians 4:1-8 and Titus 1:9?

_____

_____

_____

_____

_____

_____

Are you afraid to contradict another's viewpoint that contradicts God's Word? What makes you afraid?

_____

_____

_____

_____

_____

_____

Read I Peter 3:15 then take a moment and write down the argument you would use to show them what God says is sin.

_____

_____

_____

_____

_____

_____

_____

The Young Armor-Bearer

I Am with You Heart and Soul

I Samuel 14:7

Blondin was a famous French aerialist, one of the finest tight-rope walkers of all time. He is best known as being the man who walked a wire across Niagara Falls. On that famous crossing, there were crowds of people watching in breathless terror as Blondin maneuvered across the wire and back again. When he finally returned to the American side, he was met with throngs of praises and cheers saying, "You are the greatest, Blondin." You can do anything." "No one in the world is as great as you!"

When the cheering subsided, Blondin thanked the people and then offered them a challenge. "You say I am the greatest. Good. Then I should have no trouble getting someone to volunteer for my next act!" He said, "I need someone to ride atop my shoulders as I cross back over the Falls one more time."

The crowd went silent.

"Just one person, please," he shouted.

After a very long pause, one lone man stepped forward and climbed upon Blondin's shoulders. Then he and that lone man headed across the Falls.

Forty-five minutes later, both returned to the American side having written their names into history – a great talent and a great faith.[2]

Saul was still early in his reign as the king of Israel when his son, Prince Jonathan, attacked the Philistine garrison at Geba. This meant war! In I Samuel 13, we read that Saul had 3,000 troops at his side. But the Philistines responded:

I Samuel 13:5 (ESV)
And the Philistines mustered to fight with Israel, thirty thousand chariots and six thousand horsemen and troops like the sand on the seashore in multitude.

The Philistines were the advanced technological society. They had mastered the making of iron weapons and had mobile weapons called chariots. Israel would not have chariots until the time of Solomon. On the other hand, Israel was an agricultural society and did not even possess swords or spears. They had hunting instruments like slings and the bow & arrow. In fact, the Bible tells us that only two swords existed in the entire nation of Israel at this time.

I Samuel 13:22 (ESV)
So on the day of the battle there was neither sword nor spear found in the hand of any of the people with Saul and Jonathan, but Saul and Jonathan his son had them.

This doesn't sound like a good way to try to win a battle. And when the two sides lined up and the Israelites saw the vast army and weapons of their adversaries, many fled, hid, or switched sides. Saul was soon left with only a small force.

---

2 • Adapted from folk tales about Blondin's crossings, Abbott, K. (2011, October 18). *The Daredevil of Niagara Falls.* Smithsonian Magazine., and Graham, L. (2024, June 1). *Blondin the Hero of Niagara.* American Heritage (americanheritage.com). (Originally published in American Heritage Magazine August 1958 Vol 9. Issue 5.)

I Samuel 13:15b (ESV)
*And Saul numbered the people who were
present with him, about six hundred men.*

The odds didn't look too good in favor of the Israelites from a human perspective. But that is when God is at His best. Have you ever noticed in your life that God often seems to wait or delays His intervention until the last moment? Think about it for a moment. Moses didn't cross the Red Sea until Pharaoh was upon him. Hezekiah did not get the Lord's help until 185,000 Assyrians surrounded him. Shadrach, Meshach, and Abed-nego did not get delivered until they were put into the fiery furnace. Elijah did not heal the widow's son until after the boy died. We could go on and on with other examples.

King Saul did nothing now except sit opposite the Philistines. This stalemate went on for several days, and then the story continues.

I Samuel 14:1-15 (ESV)
*One day Jonathan the son of Saul said to the young man
who carried his armor, "Come, let us go over to the Philistine
garrison on the other side." But he did not tell his father. Saul
was staying in the outskirts of Gibeah in the pomegranate
cave at Migron. The people who were with him were about
six hundred men... [3b]And the people did not know that
Jonathan had gone. Within the passes, by which Jonathan
sought to go over to the Philistine garrison, there was a
rocky crag on the one side and a rocky crag on the other
side... [6] Jonathan said to the young man who carried
his armor, "Come, let us go over to the garrison of these
uncircumcised. It may be that the LORD will work for us,
for nothing can hinder the LORD from saving by many or
by few." And his armor-bearer said to him, "Do all that is in
your heart. Do as you wish. Behold, I am with you heart and
soul." Then Jonathan said, "Behold, we will cross over to the
men, and we will show ourselves to them. If they say to us,
'Wait until we come to you,' then we will stand still in our
place, and we will not go up to them. But if they say, 'Come
up to us,' then we will go up, for the LORD has given them*

*into our hand. And this shall be the sign to us." So both of
them showed themselves to the garrison of the Philistines.
And the Philistines said, "Look, Hebrews are coming out
of the holes where they have hidden themselves." And the
men of the garrison hailed Jonathan and his armor-bearer
and said, "Come up to us, and we will show you a thing."
And Jonathan said to his armor-bearer, "Come up after me,
for the LORD has given them into the hand of Israel." Then
Jonathan climbed up on his hands and feet, and his armor-
bearer after him. And they fell before Jonathan, and his
armor-bearer killed them after him. And that first strike,
which Jonathan and his armor-bearer made, killed about
twenty men within as it were half a furrow's length in an
acre of land. And there was a panic in the camp, in the field,
and among all the people. The garrison and even the raiders
trembled, the earth quaked, and it became a very great panic.*

Have you ever thought about this young lad who followed Prince Jonathan into battle at overwhelming odds? Oh, to have a follower who will gladly follow even when the battle seems impossible. Let's examine this young, nameless man and see what we can learn and apply to our life from his story.

First, what is an armor-bearer? It is a term to describe a personal servant who carried additional weapons for commanders or kings. Their primary duty was to follow along behind their master and slaughter the wounded that were still living after fighting. Usually, the master would have a sword or a spear as a weapon, while the armor-bearer often had just a club to dispatch those wounded. It seems that not long after the time of King David, armor-bearers became obsolete.

The first thing that stands out about Jonathan's armor-bearer is that he was young. Since he is nameless in history, we shall call him Arnold for identity purposes. Arnold didn't have years of experience in battle or military matters, but he did have confidence in his leader – Prince Jonathan. Jonathan obviously had confidence in Arnold, too.

Arnold had probably signed on or had been chosen by Jonathan to be his armor-bearer, but he probably never realized that his master would lead him into a fight where the odds were so stacked against them. Even so, Arnold followed Jonathan into this one-sided battle as brave as anyone at the Alamo. His commitment was unfailing. For instance, look at the comment he made when asked by his master to go into this battle.

I Samuel 14:7 (ESV)
And his armor-bearer said to him, "Do all that is in your heart. Do as you wish. Behold, I am with you heart and soul."

Arnold had made a commitment to Jonathan in his job. He would follow him into battle. However, this seems to be more than he had originally signed up for. Two against hundreds doesn't seem quite fair. But Arnold didn't say to Jonathan, "Are you nuts? Look at all those men over there. They aren't smiling and they have real weapons, not like this tree branch I'm carrying!" And Arnold didn't say, "Whoa, Jonathan. I didn't sign up for this. If you want to commit suicide, fine. But leave me out of it!" Arnold didn't tell Jonathan, "You go ahead, but I need to run to Walmart and buy a gun first." Nor did Arnold say, "I really don't feel like doing that today. I sort of have this cough and a headache. You go ahead and I'm sure someone else will come and help you." Arnold didn't even say, "You go first, and I'll come along later when it is safe."

No, what Arnold did say is, "I am with you heart and soul." Others had signed on to fight in this army, but they were either hiding, or lazy, or traitors. Our hero went into battle armed with nothing more than just a club. He went right away too. He didn't hesitate about what his job was. This man was committed to his master, his job, and his God. The size of the opposition didn't matter to him. He was quite willing to use the resources he had at hand. In short, what Arnold said was, "I'll follow you and fulfill my obligation. I told you I would defend you and I will go with you wherever and whenever you say."

As I examine Arnold, I notice some key characteristics that he possessed. First, he was vigilant. He was watchful and alert to the danger facing him, but he had trust in Jonathan and God Who told him that no problem is too great.

Second, he had self-control. Facing a large enemy in combat is a terrifying thing. I recall my dad who fought in WWII telling me of one battle when he and his comrades were attacked one night by a Japanese banzai charge. "They stormed our lines and kept coming until they finally broke through, and it became hand-to-hand combat. Biting, spitting, punching, and stabbing. Finally, the Japanese were all killed." He told me that it is hard to describe the feeling you get when you see scores of enemy soldiers charging you. He said that it takes self-control and trust in your buddy to stay there and fight. Arnold knew what that was like.

Third, Arnold made himself do the hard thing. It would have been so easy to go and hide or be lazy like the rest of the army that was sitting around doing nothing. But he realized his commitment and made the decision to be there on time and do what he was supposed to do. Today, we find too many people coming to work late or more concerned about their own comfort. They don't think much of their commitment. This causes some people to think of Christians as being lazy. But Christians should remember who they are working for:

Colossians 3:23 (ESV)
Whatever you do, work heartily,
as for the Lord and not for men.

Fourth, Arnold exchanged comfort, warmth, and safety for God's work. Comfort, warmth, and safety are human desires and sometimes those desires of the flesh should be crucified on the cross of Christ. These three items can become a crutch that hinders our walk and duty to God.

Yes, I am impressed with this young Arnold. If we compare him to the supposed real leader of Israel, King Saul, we see some amazing differences.

KING SAUL	JONATHAN & ARNOLD
Sat around doing nothing	Attacked an over-whelming force
Trusted in his army alone	Trusted in God alone
A watcher who did nothing	A doer
Impressed people with talk and oaths	His actions impressed people
All talk and no action	Big actions, big victories
Weakened the army	Encouraged the army

So how do you compare with our hero Arnold? Are you vigilant in your duties? Are you self-controlled in your work ethic? Can you deny your human flesh and stay the course for God? Are you willing to exchange comforts of this life for service for God? Are you willing to use whatever God has given you to work for His Kingdom? Or are you someone who has accepted a challenge or a duty but fails to complete it or to even do it with all of your heart? If so, what kind of witness are you of our Lord Jesus Christ?

During July of 1863, General Robert E. Lee of the Confederacy invaded Pennsylvania. In those days of warfare, the cavalry units were the "eyes and ears" of the army. As General Lee was invading the north, he needed to know where the Northern Army was and its strength. He gave this job to the young and flamboyant General Jeb Stuart. As Lee proceeded northward, Stuart was to supply him with intelligence on the enemy's position and strength. But Lee heard nothing from Stuart. Weeks passed with no word whatsoever of the whereabouts of the Union. Suddenly, on July 3rd, Union General Buford's cavalry unit came face-to-face with part of Lee's army in the little city of Gettysburg. Lee's army could have easily been surrounded by the Union forces, but the resourceful Lee and General Longstreet routed the Union back.

Midway through this battle, General Stuart came riding into Lee's headquarters. Lee delayed meeting with Stuart until late one evening during the battle. When at last Stuart was allowed to meet with Lee, Lee told him that many of the other officers felt like Stuart had let them down. He continued by saying that it was an act of God that the entire army was not destroyed, because he had no idea of the Union strength or location.

Jeb Stuart then pulled out his sword and tried to hand it to Lee saying that since he had lost faith in his ability to do his job, he was resigning. Lee yelled back that there was no time for this type of behavior. Calming himself, Lee handed back Stuarts's sword saying that he still believed that he was one of the finest cavalry officers in the army and that the South still needed him. He continued by softly telling Stuart that he had failed not only Lee but the Cause. Then Lee stated bluntly, "But this will never happen again." He repeated softly that Stuart must be sure that this will never happen again. Then he turned and said to him, "Let us speak no more on this matter."

Tears came to Jeb Stuart's eyes as he realized that he had let down not only his commander and fellow officers and had failed at his duty, but he also let down the man he admired the most.

Fan the Flame

Have you ever accepted a job or agreed to do something only to discover it wasn't what you thought it would be? Describe the situation.

What did you do when you found out?

Was your performance affected? In what way?

How were you viewed by your peers, your "boss"? How did your performance affect others?

Read Colossians 3:17, 23, 24 and write down what God expects of you.

What can/could you do to reconcile the situation in accordance to God's will?

Shamgar
God Can Use Anyone He Chooses

Judges 3:31

Back in the 1980s I was hired by a school in Illinois to give some guidance to their science department. The students' ACT scores in science were extremely low. I had just finished working at another school where I overhauled their curriculum, and the school was recognized for excellence in this area. Now I was looking for another place to work and this small school in Illinois was interested in me. During the interview process I told the school principal and the superintendent that if in three years the ACT scores in science were not doubled, I would resign. However, the success of the program would depend on them providing money for supplies as well as giving me complete control of the department. It was agreed and I was excited about my new job.

During the time I worked at this school, I tried many new ideas in education and I rewrote their biology curriculum. Things were progressing very well after the first year. But during the second year I noticed that the school had many remedial students. I was intrigued by this and began trying some way to counter this problem.

About this time, I began taking some classes at SIU-Carbondale to help me become a better teacher and to discover new trends in education. One of the professors was Dr. Applebee. He introduced me to a new concept in education called teaching across the curriculum. This was a new trend that required teachers to teach other subjects in their classes. For example, he challenged me to teach more reading, grammar, math, etc. in my biology classes. Thus, I began teaching reading in my biology classes utilizing newspapers and magazines that contained articles dealing with various areas of biology I happened to be covering at the time. For instance, I found an article in Glamour magazine on bacterial infections people could get from sitting in saunas. I called Glamour for permission to copy and utilize their article in my classroom which they granted me. The students read the article and wrote a synopsis or abstract on a 3x5 card. I assigned these weekly in my classes, and surprisingly, the students loved these and often asked me for more assignments like this.

At about this same time, I concluded that some of the remedial students were incapable of reading and comprehending a high school textbook. I had some of them tested by the guidance department on reading and found that one student could not read a 4th grade reader. I began tutoring this student as well as integrating more reading into my classes. I and my students were happy with these new ideas, but someone was not.

During the middle of my third year, I was called into the principal's office after school. Waiting for me was the chair of the English department and the superintendent of the school district among others. I was then interrogated about teaching reading in my classes. The English chair was furious with me. I was told to stop all reading assignments and activities as this was her department. I tried to explain that I was trying to help because we had so many students that were below their reading levels. The superintendent told me to let her teach reading while I focused on my own subject. I then foolishly exclaimed, "But she is not teaching reading! Some of these kids can't read the textbook!" This was a mistake and just made matters worse. I lost the battle in the office. Fortunately for me, I was offered a new position at a different school district that spring that welcomed my ideas.

As I look back upon this experience, I saw a need that was not being filled. All I did was try to help. True, it was not my stated job to teach reading, but not much was being done to help correct this problem.

Sometimes people will find themselves living in a situation that is problematic, where things are not moving in the direction that they should. They could ignore the problem, thinking that someone more qualified than themselves should step up and make the necessary changes. On the other hand, instead of ignoring the problem, they could take a stand and try to make changes. This takes courage. It means moving outside the comfort zone to do what is right, regardless of what others may think. Christians are often too timid or nonchalant in addressing the failings of church leadership. They commonly state, "Let the pastor do it! It is his job, not mine!" In this lesson, we will read of a person who was the least likely to be used by God to make changes, yet he stepped up to the challenge. His name is Shamgar.

After the Exodus and Joshua's Conquest was the period of the Judges. It was a time before the monarchy of David and an age of lawlessness. In fact, the era was defined in Judges 17:6:

Judges 17:6 (ESV)
In those days there was no king in Israel.
Everyone did what was right in his own eyes.

It was sort of reminiscent of the American Wild West. There was no king of Israel at this time. Without a strong leader, the people fell into idol worship and forgot the God of their fathers. This allowed the neighboring nations to invade and oppress the Israelites.

Judges 2:14-15 (ESV)
So the anger of the LORD was kindled against Israel, and he
gave them over to plunderers, who plundered them. And
he sold them into the hand of their surrounding enemies,
so that they could no longer withstand their enemies.
Whenever they marched out, the hand of the LORD was
against them for harm, as the LORD had warned, and as the
Lord had sworn to them. And they were in terrible distress.

Then they would cry out to God, and He would raise up a Judge to lead them.

Judges 2:16 (ESV)
Then the LORD raised up judges, who saved them
out of the hand of those who plundered them.

What's a Judge? The Hebrew word for this is שָׁפַט **shaphat**, which means to pronounce sentence, litigate, or to govern. A Judge was the leader of the Israelites at this time in history. The Bible names the Judges during the era following Joshua's death to the last Judge, Samuel. Then the people demanded a king. God gave them Saul; therefore the period of the Judges was over.

Some of the Judges were amazing people. Some were major players doing remarkable jobs, while others were minor characters in which little information is given. There were six major Judges and six minor Judges.

The first Judge was Othniel, nephew to Caleb; the same Caleb who was one of the spies sent by Moses into the Promise Land during the Exodus and came back with an optimistic report. Othniel is mentioned in Judges 3:7-11.

The second Judge was Ehud from the Tribe of Benjamin. He led Israel into battle against the Moabites who were oppressing Israel. His exploits are recorded in Judge 3:15-30.

The next major Judge was Deborah who fought against King Jabin and the Canaanites. Her feats are recorded in Judges 4-5.

But wait! We missed someone. Shamgar was also a Judge and governed between Ehud and Deborah. He was only given two verses in the entire Bible. The only verse that really describes him is Judges 3:31.

Judges 3:31 (ESV)
After him was Shamgar the son of Anath, who killed 600 of
the Philistines with an oxgoad, and he also saved Israel.

Shamgar is one of those literally forgotten Bible heroes that we hardly ever hear about. Let's explore this minor character and see what God can teach us from his story. Even though this verse is but one sentence, we can learn something of major importance from him. But to do this, we must first dissect this verse. In doing so, we see some facts about this man.

First, Shamgar's name itself. It is not Hebrew at all. It is a Canaanite name, which tells us that he is a foreigner and not even an Israelite! Doesn't that seem strange to you? There are many Israelites in the country, yet God uses this Canaanite to lead His people instead! That is amazing.

This leads us to ask some questions such as: Why didn't God choose to use an Israelite? Was there no Israelite walking closely with God after Ehud's death? Where were all the men from the Tribe of Judah, the Tribe that was supposed to be leading Israel? Where were the Levite men who were supposed to be God's ministers and representatives? Why didn't the High Priest come forward and lead the people? This questioning can go on and on. I find it so amazing that not one Israelite, who was supposed to be fulfilling this role, came forward to do the job. It saddens my heart, but I am sure it saddened God's even more.

Second, Shamgar was the son of Anath. Well, that sounds nice; but if one researches Anath, one finds something very interesting again. Anath was a goddess the Canaanites worshipped. She was the goddess of war and a chief god of the Ugarite people of northern Syria. She was a consort of Baal. Some scholars believe that this Anath is another name for one of the Ashtars, a group of deities worshipped in Canaan, but commonly called Asherah in the Bible.

Some other scholars believe that Anath refers to the Canaanite god of irrigation, but little is known about this god. One more thing that is interesting about this name is that Anath is a feminine name. This would indicate that the Anath mentioned in Judges was probably Shamgar's mother. In any case, Shamgar was from a family that appears to have been involved in Anath worship sometime in its past. This makes this Judge even more extraordinary than originally thought; he possibly came from a family dedicated to idol worship. But whatever the case, when Shamgar became Israel's Judge, he was a follower of Elohim or YHWH.

According to scholars, Canaanite worship of Anath and Asherah involved sexual orgies. It was a sensual religion involving male and female prostitutes who acted as priests and priestesses having relations with worshipers. If Shamgar's mother was involved in this worship as a prostitute, which many scholars believe, she could have been impregnated by some unknown man. Thus, the identity of Shamgar's father would be a mystery. Ac-

Images of Anath found at Lachish, Israel Museum (E4F)

cordingly, either Shamgar's mother or Shamgar himself broke away from this idol worship for the true God of Israel.

There is another theory about this Anath. Some believe it was a small town in northern Naphtali called Beth-Anath, meaning that Shamgar came from here. But this idea is not popular with most Bible scholars or archaeologists.

Third, he fought against the Philistines and routed them by killing 600 of them. Israel had indeed turned again from God and was worshiping foreign idols. This being the case, God allowed the Philistines to oppress the Israelites. The Philistines were a sea people that migrated from Greece and settled in the south

Canaan area. If Shamgar did indeed come from Naphtali, this would indicate that the Philistines had conquered many square miles of Israeli territory, since the Philistines dwelt in the southern area and Naphtali was up in the north.

Fourth, Shamgar wars with and kills 600 Philistines using an ox goad. What is an ox goad? The word is actually a compound word. An ox is of course a beast of burden that was common in the agricultural nation of Israel. A goad is what a plowman used to urge the ox to move. It was a long stick, approximately 7-8 feet in length and having a point at one end. This point was usually tipped with iron and sharpened. So, an ox goad was something very similar to a spear.

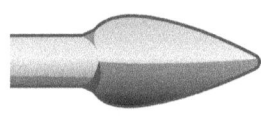

Approximate shape of the point of an oxgoad.

An ox goad would certainly be a formidable weapon, but it also tells us another interesting part to this story. Shamgar was a farmer and made do with what was available. He did not make a dagger as the previous Judge Ehud had done. He made use and in this case, warred with what he had at hand.

Fifth, Shamgar was the savior of Israel. The Philistines had been oppressing them, but Shamgar appears to have stopped this entirely with one major action. The Bible does not go into details of a military campaign here as it does with other Judges, but it does tell us that Shamgar got to work and accomplished his goal right away. His victory over the Philistines was so complete that it ended the Philistine occupation. The next enemy that Israel faced was a combined military army composed of Canaanite nations, not the Philistines.

What can we learn from God about our walk with Him from this one verse in the Bible concerning Shamgar?

First, God can use anyone He chooses. In this case, there were plenty of people who should have come forward to do God's calling, but it took a foreigner to do the job. I am sure there were people still loyal to God in Israel who said that they could be the Judge, but when words turned to action, no one stepped forward. We often see the same thing today. Plenty of people say that they will manage others for God and serve Him, but when words aren't enough and action is needed, few ever come forward. Haven't you ever noticed that in most of our churches today just a few people who are often overly involved in other ministries execute the majority of work being performed there? Most of the Church seems quite content to allow someone else to do the job, even if no one comes forward. Too many Christians today are stuck to their pews or chairs and just can't get their bodies in gear to do something for God. No wonder the Church today sees so many of its active members experience burnout.

Second, Shamgar was not an Israelite. He did not go to David Theological Seminary, but he was not afraid to take over when an Israelite would not step forward to do their job. We need to be willing to step in when a need arises. Wherever you are, if you see a void in God's work that someone else was supposed to fill, yet no one comes forward, be a Shamgar and just do it. God will get the glory from it, and you will be blessed.

Third, Shamgar did not use a real weapon. He led Israel into battle with a farming tool, an ox goad. He used what was available to him to accomplish God's goal. He obtained victory by using what he had. You, too, can work for God using what is at hand. You don't have to look for something special to do God's work. He will equip you or enable you to use whatever is at hand.

Back in the early 1990s I was teaching at one the best schools in Illinois. One reason the school was so good was that it was blessed with the best principal I have ever met. Bill Freeman was not only a gifted and brilliant principal, but he was also a master teacher.

One day during lunchtime, I was taking a walk around the hallways. By chance I saw Bill walking in my direction. We met and walked together for some distance. I can still recall him telling me that he was most impressed that I had taken my environmental biology students snorkeling in one of the school ponds for a class. He then commented on a few other things that he admired in my teaching. (Bill knew how to encourage his teachers.) We stopped at a junction near the cafeteria, and he asked me what goals I had in mind for the science department. As I was telling him a big idea of mine, he started to walk away from me. At first I kept talking, but then I stopped speaking and wondered what I said that made him just walk away like I wasn't there. I studied him as he walked about 15-20 feet down the hall, paused, bent over, and picked up a small, penny-sized piece of paper off the floor. He then walked a few more steps to a trashcan where he deposited the wastepaper. Afterwards, he came walking back to me to where he originally stood and then asked, "Now where were we?" I was flabbergasted. I asked him why he walked over to get that piece of paper when the custodian, who was pushing a large broom further down the hall, could easily have swept it up. He told me that he just wanted to help him. He said that maybe he might miss it. "Besides", he continued, "Don't you think it is good to help in areas other than your own?"

I am sure that Bill forgot this event, but it is still so vivid in my mind. He taught me that even if someone else is assigned to a task, I could still help. In some cases, the person assigned does not do the task, and that leaves me to do it.

Fan the Flame

Have you ever seen a need you felt was not being addressed? What was it? Did you do anything to solve it?

Make a list of needs you see that no one appears to be addressing:

Next to each need, write what you feel is needed to take care of the need.

Think about whether you can help fulfill the need with what is available to you. Remember to think "outside of the box."

Read Hebrews 13:20-22. You can supply what is needed. Rewrite the verses in a concise statement as though it is written directly to you.

The Oracle
of Philippi
Hearing the Word of God

Acts 16:16-24

The Bible can change not only a life but an entire lifestyle. Most of us have heard the story of the Mutiny on the Bounty, but few of us have heard how the Bible played an extremely vital part in that historical event.

The Bounty was a British ship, which set sail from England in 1787, bound for the South Seas. The idea was that those on board would spend some time among the islands, transplanting fruit-bearing and producing trees, and doing other things to make some of the islands more habitable. After ten months of voyage, the Bounty arrived safely at its destination, and for six months the officers and the crew gave themselves to the duties placed upon them by their government.

When the special task was completed, however, and the order came to embark again, the sailors rebelled. They had formed strong attachments with the native girls, and the climate and the ease of the South Sea Island life were much to their liking. The result was mutiny on the Bounty, and the sailors placed Captain Bligh and a few loyal men adrift in an open boat. Captain Bligh, in an almost miraculous fashion, survived the ordeal, was rescued, and eventually arrived home in London to tell his story. An expedition was launched to punish the mutineers, and in due time fourteen of them were captured and paid the penalty under British law.

However, nine of the men had gone to another distant island and formed a colony. Perhaps there has never been a more degraded and debauched social life than that colony. They learned how to distill whiskey from a native plant, and the whiskey, with other habits, led to their ruin. Disease and murder took the lives of all the native men and all but one of the white men. The lone survivor was Alexander Smith. He found himself the only man on the island, surrounded by a crowd of women and mixed race children. Alexander Smith found a Bible among the possessions of a dead sailor. Although the Book was new to him, he read it and believed. He read the Bible and taught classes about it to the women and children because he wanted others to share in the benefits of the Scriptures as well.

It was twenty years before a ship ever found that island, and when it did, a miniature Utopia was discovered. The people were living in decency, prosperity, harmony, and peace. There was nothing of crime, disease, immorality, insanity, or illiteracy. How was it accomplished? By the reading, the believing, and the appropriation of the truth of God.[3]

Jews and Christians are very fortunate indeed compared to worldly religions, especially those of the ancient world. That is because the Jews were the chosen people of God through whom He gave His Word. And since we Christians were borne out of the Jewish roots, we, too, have access to the actual Word of God. No other nation on earth was so blessed yet held so responsible than the Jews and Christians.

---

3 • Swindoll, C. R. (1998). Bible-Influence Of. In *Swindoll's Ultimate book of illustrations & quotes: Over 1,500 outstanding ways to effectively drive home your message* (pp. 50–51). T. Nelson. // Miller, K., & Larson, B. (1977). Bible. In *The Edge of Adventure: An Experiment in Faith* (pp. 70). Word Books.

This was not the case in the ancient world of Greece and Rome. To hear the word of the gods or to find answers to questions for just about everything from daily living to career choices, it was difficult to ascertain what the gods indeed thought or wished. These gentiles did not have an inspired, written word from their deities. To understand this, we will need to look back in history to a time when people were trying to discover the will of the gods.

In the ancient world of the Greek & Roman Empires, the word of the gods was not written down upon scrolls or tablets for people to access. They were required to go to the temples of the gods and personally ask the priests for answers to their questions.

The most sought after god for determining the path of their lives was Apollo. Besides being the god of light and music, he was the god of oracle. An oracle was a message from the gods and also referred to the person giving the message to others. An oracle was one who gave a word from the gods to the people. Generally, it was protocol to ask a question. If you asked the gods a question such as, "If I do this, what will happen?" An oracle would then reply, "If you do (such and such), then this will happen." But it did not necessarily mean that it was the definitive future. It was simply a response to the question. The oracle would tell what the result would be if someone followed a certain course of action. Thus, in a way it was like fortune telling. The message or oracle came from the underworld. According to this religion, Apollo had connections with the underworld and was able to give answers to his followers concerning what would happen if they followed a certain course of action. But Apollo did not have temples in many cities. The major temples to Apollo were in:

- Delphi, Greece, which is about an 80-mile journey from both Athens and Corinth. A premiere temple whose priests were also sent to other temples.

- Didyma, in present Turkey, the second largest temple in the ancient world.

- Bassae, in western Greece. This temple sat in a north-south direction because of the mountaintop it was built upon, making it rather unique.

Temple of Apollo, Delphi, Greece (Jason M Ramos / Wikimedia, CC BY 2.0)

*Temples of Apollo in (left) Corinth, Greece (Ploync / Wikimedia, CC BY 3.0)
and (right) Athens, Greece (Jacob Freeland / Wikimedia, CC BY 4.0)*

- Gortyna, on the island of Crete.
- Siracusa, on the island of Sicily.
- Miletus, in present-day Turkey.

Thus, to find out the will of Apollo, they had to go to his temple and ask his priest. To do this, they had to make some major sacrifices:

- They had to plan out the trip including lodging and food expenses.
- They had to take time off work for a long period of time. This could sometimes run into months.
- They had to have money on hand for other expenses.

Temple of Apollo, Didyma, Turkey (Frunze103 / Wikimedia, CC0)

- They had to purchase a sheep that would be sacrificed to see if the gods would answer their question.

- They had to bring things to occupy their time while awaiting an answer.

Once there at the temple, it is believed that they would follow something like this procedure:

1. Wash at the holy well to purify themselves.

2. Have a priest wash their sheep.

3. Have the priest slaughter the sheep and examine its liver to see if the gods would hear their question.

4. Go into the oracle door in the temple if they were approved.

5. Wait until a priest would open the doors from the inside to hear their question. (This was done with great drama and fanfare.)

6. Watch as the doors were opened, and the priest, dressed up like Apollo, would stand in the doorway and shout, "Apollo will hear your question."

Temple of Apollo, Bassae, Greece (Rijksmuseum / Wikimedia, CC0)

Temples of Apollo in (left) Gortyna, Crete (Mark Landon / Wikimedia, CC BY 4.0) and (right) Siracusa, Sicily (amanderson2 / Wikimedia, CC BY 2.0)

7. Bow before the priest and then present their question to him.

8. Remain at the doorway as the priest would go back inside, and the doors would be closed.

9. Waited, sometimes for months on end. Some people played games on the floor of the temple.

The following took place inside the inner temple while they waited:

1. The priest would write their question on a tablet and give it to the oracle. She was called a Pythia. According to Greek Mythology, the Pythian was a serpent or dragon that dwelled in Pytho, at the foot of mount Parnassus. It guard-

ed the oracle there and was killed by Apollo. After this event, the name was transferred to Apollo, and he would speak to certain maidens that were then called a Pythian. Apollo would speak to the Pythia if she was a virgin and had fasted. (In earlier times, she would be a young virgin, but in later times they used an old woman. The change was due to men kidnapping or having sex with the young virgin and then she was no longer any use to them.)

2. The oracle would be suspended over a fissure in the earth. This fissure had fumes coming up from the underworld. These fumes were probably a combination of methane, ethane, and ethylene – which has a sweet odor. They would induce a trance-like state and possibly alter the sound of her voice. These gases could make the girl intoxicated or stoned.

3. The oracle would receive the question and sometimes recite some gibberish, which the priest standing nearby would decipher and write down on a tablet as "the answer."

4. The priest returned to the doorway to proclaim the word of Apollo to them.

5. Having found their answer, they returned home.

That was quite a bit of work just to hear the word of the gods or to know what the god's will was for various situations.

Now to the Jews, this was a detestable thing. God explicitly told the Jews not to seek information from the underworld or from demons.

Deuteronomy 18:10-11 (ESV)
There shall not be found among you anyone who
burns his son or his daughter as an offering, anyone who
practices divination or tells fortunes or interprets omens,
or a sorcerer or a charmer or a medium or a wizard
or a necromancer or one who inquires of the dead

Leviticus 19 tells us that God detested false oracles and false seers.

Leviticus 19:31 (ESV)
"Do not turn to mediums or necromancers;
do not seek them out, and so make yourselves
unclean by them: I am the LORD your God.

But God was not against all oracles, just false ones. He uses the term oracle Himself for His Word. Malachi begins with:

Malachi 1:1 (ESV)
The oracle of the word of the LORD to Israel by Malachi.

You see the word oracle is not a bad word. Eighteen times in the Old Testament and at least twice in the New Testament the Word of God is referred to as an oracle. Often it is phrased something like "the Word of the Lord came to Elijah…"

Now, with that information, let's begin our character study. Paul and Silas were on their second missionary journey and had come to the Macedonian city of Philippi. While in this city, a strange encounter unfolded.

Acts 16:16-24 (ESV)
As we were going to the place of prayer, we were met by
a slave girl who had a spirit of divination and brought
her owners much gain by fortune-telling. She followed
Paul and us, crying out, "These men are servants of
the Most High God, who proclaim to you the way of
salvation." And this she kept doing for many days. Paul,
having become greatly annoyed, turned and said to
the spirit, "I command you in the name of Jesus Christ
to come out of her." And it came out that very hour.

But when her owners saw that their hope of gain was
gone, they seized Paul and Silas and dragged them into the
marketplace before the rulers. And when they had brought
them to the magistrates, they said, "These men are Jews,
and they are disturbing our city. They advocate customs
that are not lawful for us as Romans to accept or practice."
The crowd joined in attacking them, and the magistrates

tore the garments off them and gave orders to beat them with rods. And when they had inflicted many blows upon them, they threw them into prison, ordering the jailer to keep them safely. Having received this order, he put them into the inner prison and fastened their feet in the stocks.

I have always been a bit puzzled by this passage in the Bible. Why did God give us this story? Why would a riot emerge in the city from one girl losing her power to tell the future? Jesus expelled many demons from people without causing a riot. Even other disciples and apostles cast out demons without causing an uproar. So why did this one instance cause a massive disturbance in Philippi? The reason is now understandable. They just didn't shut the mouth of a demon-possessed girl, but they extinguished the voice of their gods! This was a very serious crime to these gentiles because Paul and Silas were responsible for silencing the voice of Apollo!

In her case, she was a demon-possessed oracle. She was probably the oracle of Apollo in the city. The people could no longer go to her for the oracle. The convenience of having a Pythia in Philippi was gone. The people of Philippi no longer had easy access to the word of the gods. According to Vine's Dictionary:

> *The passage in Acts 16:16 has the term divination. This word in ancient Greek was* **Πύθων puthon** *(Eng., "python") "pu thone" in Greek mythology was the name of the Pythian serpent or dragon, dwelling in Pytho, at the foot of mount Parnassus, guarding the oracle of Delphi, and slain by Apollo. Thence the name was transferred to Apollo himself. Later the word was applied to diviners or soothsayers, regarded as inspired by Apollo. Since demons are the agents inspiring idolatry, 1 Corinthians 10:20, the young woman in Acts 16:16 was possessed by a demon instigating the cult of Apollo, and thus had "a spirit of divination."*[4]

---

4 • W. Vine, M.F. Unger, & W. White, (1996). *Vine's Complete Expository Dictionary of Old and New Testament Words.* T.Nelson

What can we learn from this study? The thing that strikes me most is what the people had to do to hear the word of the gods. Compare that to Christians today. We do not have to travel to a temple. We do not have to wash our bodies. We do not have to wash a sheep, slaughter it, and examine its liver. We do not have to wait for months to be able to hear the oracle of God. We have **THE WORD OF GOD!**

But let me ask you, when was the last time you read a passage in the Word of God? When was the last time you read a chapter in the Word of God? How many times do I hear people say that they want to be a disciple of Christ but can't find the time to read the Word of God! Do we really want to be disciples of Jesus? Then why can't we get up 10 minutes earlier in our day to read our Bibles? **To be a disciple is to be a man or a woman of the oracle of God – His Word – His Text!** If you are sitting here right now saying to yourself that you want to be a true follower and disciple of Jesus, yet don't have the time to read the Word, I must ask you – "How badly do you want to be a disciple of Jesus?!"

There is a story I once heard about an old icehouse. Back in the days before electric refrigerators were invented, people would store ice in a building called an icehouse. These were often constructed of wood and thickly insulated with sawdust. In fact, my father once worked in an icehouse in southern Illinois when he was a boy. He said that the owners would cut blocks of ice out of the frozen lakes and rivers during the winter and store them in the icehouse with sawdust covering them. He told me that even in the hot days of summer, he could go into the icehouse and pull out a block of ice that was stored there six months earlier.

In this story, a man who was working in an icehouse lost his valuable watch in the sawdust. He searched and searched, but with no success. He called his fellow workers and together they all searched for that lost watch, but no one found it.

That night, a young boy heard about the lost watch in the dark icehouse. He got permission to search and after an hour or so, he came out holding the watch in his hands. When asked how he found it so quickly, he said that it was simple. He laid down on the sawdust and listened for the ticking of the watch. In the quiet icehouse, he heard the watch ticking, crawled over, and pulled it out of the sawdust.[5]

There is a spiritual lesson here for us. To find the watch, the boy tried to hear the watch ticking. To do this he had to be quiet and let it "speak" to him. Then he found it by the sounds it was making. Are you searching for an oracle from God? You don't have to go far, just sit down with His Word and search with diligence while quietly listening to His oracle.

Fan the Flame

At the beginning of this chapter, you read how people's lives were changed for the better after a man started reading and teaching from a Bible he found. You then went on to read how Greeks and Romans would seek out answers to life by visiting temples and asking a god for answers. Let's look at some Bible verses to explain why the Bible contains answers to your questions.

How can we find and know the Word of God? By understanding what that Word is. Read the first chapter of the Gospel of John. Read it slowly and let the words sink deeply. Just who is this Word? Look at verse 14. The Word is flesh and blood! Read I John 1:1-4. The same man wrote both books, the apostle John. In the short epistle/letter from John he clearly states that he physically saw, touched, and spoke with this Word of God.

---

5 • Rowell, E. K. (2007). Illustrations. In *1001 Quotes, Illustrations & Humorous Stories for preachers, teachers, & writers* (pp. 279). Baker Books.

According to Acts 1:9-11, Jesus no longer physically lives on earth but will return at some point in the future. So how can we get answers from Him? By studying what God has to say. The Holy Spirit is given to all followers of Jesus and His job is to teach us. Write down what John 14:26 says about the Holy Spirit.

The Bible contains 66 individual books covering the beginning of creation and mankind, history of the Jewish nation, prophecies, end times, practical living advice, and gives many, many details of the life and message of Jesus while He lived on this earth. Not everything written about God or Jesus is truthful, but you can rely on these 66 books to give you an accurate accounting of the Word of God. Why? Look at II Timothy 3:16-17. God Himself made sure of it.

Start reading the Bible and look for answers to your questions. Don't know where to start? Since there are 66 separate books in the Bible, they are not compiled in chronological order. (Chronological Bibles are available for sale.) My recommendation is to start with one of the four gospels: Matthew (a Jewish tax collector who wrote his account for fellow Jews), Mark (many scholars believe this young man wrote this gospel with the Apostle Peter), Luke (a Greek doctor who wrote this gospel as well as the book of Acts to Greeks), or John (close friend of Jesus and youngest of the apostles who also wrote I, II, and III John and the Book of Revelation). Reading at least one gospel and then the Book of Acts (a historical record of the beginning of the Christian church) will give you a good look at who this Word of God is.

Hanun

Getting Your Facts Straight

II Samuel 10:1-7

When a fellow was getting ready to travel abroad, several people warned him to watch out for pickpockets when he got to a particularly busy city. If he went down to the crowded subway, a pickpocket could grab his wallet and get on the train, the doors would shut, and the pickpocket would be gone. He determined to be very careful.

One evening after arriving in the city he was dressed casually in a sport coat, and he came to the crush of people down in the subway. Sure enough, just about the time the door opened, and some people were pouring on, a fellow bumped up against him and he thought, "That was strange." So, he reached into his pocket, and he didn't find his wallet! Well, he grabbed this fellow's coat just as the door began to close and began to pull. Finally, he got the coat all the way out even though the guy was struggling, and the door closed and the fellow inside looked bewildered as the subway train took off. Proud of himself, the guy thought, "Well, that showed him." But when he looked in the fellow's coat, he didn't find his wallet. All that for nothing! But the story had a happy ending – he found his wallet on the bureau at the hotel.[6]

---

6 • Swindoll, C. R. (1998). Mistakes. In *Swindoll's Ultimate book of illustrations & quotes: Over 1,500 outstanding ways to effectively drive home your message* (pp. 379). T. Nelson.

Let's bid welcome to a young king from yesteryear named Hanun. He was an Ammonite and the son of Nahash, a king during the times of Saul and David. The Ammonites were descendants of Abraham's nephew Lot by his incestuous relationship with his youngest daughter. Thus, they were of similar blood to the Hebrews. Even so, when the Exodus occurred, the Ammonites treated the Israelites poorly. During the period of the Judges, they invaded and fought the Israelites. King Saul fought against them. However, David found refuge with Nahash when Saul was trying to kill him. Later when David became king, Nahash had an alliance with David. So naturally, when King Nahash died, David sent ambassadors to the funeral to honor his friend. But the new young King Hanun didn't believe they had come to honor his father.

II Samuel 10:1-7 (ESV)

After this the king of the Ammonites died, and Hanun his son reigned in his place. And David said, "I will deal loyally with Hanun the son of Nahash, as his father dealt loyally with me." So David sent by his servants to console him concerning his father. And David's servants came into the land of the Ammonites. But the princes of the Ammonites said to Hanun their lord, "Do you think, because David has sent comforters to you, that he is honoring your father? Has not David sent his servants to you to search the city and to spy it out and to overthrow it?" So Hanun took David's servants and shaved off half the beard of each and cut off their garments in the middle, at their hips, and sent them away. When it was told David, he sent to meet them, for the men were greatly ashamed. And the king said, "Remain at Jericho until your beards have grown and then return." When the Ammonites saw that they had become a stench to David, the Ammonites sent and hired the Syrians of Beth-rehob, and the Syrians of Zobah, 20,000 foot soldiers, and the king of Maacah with 1,000 men, and the men of Tob, 12,000 men. And when David heard of it, he sent Joab and all the host of the mighty men.

Hanun made the mistake of his life. He assumed the worst and did not check his facts before launching his country into a disastrous situation. We look at this biblical character and say, "How could Hanun be so stupid?!" Well, it is easy to understand because we all make mistakes like Hanun did. So where did Hanun go wrong, and what can we learn from this passage that God has given to us?

We must understand that Hanun was probably under some great stress at this time. After all, his father had just died. We do not know what kind of relationship he had with his father, but he does make many poor choices as the new king. This could indicate that he was grieving over his loss. When one is overwhelmed with sadness, one often does not make wise decisions. I have witnessed this numerous times with families going through the grieving process. The stress is tremendous, and those experiencing it often don't think in rational ways. Here, Hanun makes one of the first decisions as the new king, and it is a blunder.

We can learn from this story. When we are in stressful situations and under pressure, think twice before reacting to any news. I know in my personal life that my first gut reactions are often the exact opposite of what I should do. I am learning to withdraw to a quiet place to talk with God before reacting to some news or gossip with my "gut" feelings. In those peaceful moments, the Holy Spirit often guides us by bringing Scripture verses to mind. The quiet can set our minds on the right path of common sense as well.

The second point from this passage is another major lesson for life. Look carefully at how God tells us of the major mistake Hanun makes.

II Samuel 10:3 (ESV)
But the princes of the Ammonites said to Hanun their lord, "Do you think, because David has sent comforters to you, that he is honoring your father? Has not David sent his servants to you to search the city and to spy it out and to overthrow it?"

Who was suggesting David's ambassadors are spies? It was not the court officials who were aides-de-camp to his dad, King Nahash, who ill-advised Hanun, but his peers. The guilty princes of Ammon spread rumors and gossip; Hanun foolishly allowed himself to be manipulated by them.

There is in the Law a command from God concerning gossip.

Leviticus 19:16 (ESV)
You shall not go around as a slanderer among
your people, and you shall not stand up against
the life of your neighbor: I am the LORD.

What can we learn from this aspect of the story God has given us? First, don't listen to gossip. I haven't heard of gossip ever helping a relationship, but I've often heard of the damage it causes. God even tells us in His Law not to gossip. It doesn't get any plainer than that.

Second, we can learn from Hanun where to look for advice. When searching for guidance, your peers are often as inexperienced as you are (though many think they are experts). Solomon's son King Rehoboam did the exact same thing. He did not take advice of the wise men that counseled his father but listened instead to his peers (I Kings 12:6-15).

I Kings 12:8 (ESV)
But he [Rehoboam] abandoned the counsel that the old
men gave him and took counsel with the young men
who had grown up with him and stood before him.

If you are searching for advice when you are young, you will typically get better guidance from older, wiser people than your peers. I can't help but think that the men who had advised Hanun's father Nahash must have been pulling their hair out by the roots at this rash and stupid decision the new king made.

Third, we can learn a lesson from this passage about how not to insult someone. Hanun, now convinced by his peers that David's ambassadors are there to spy on him, decides to add insult to his ruinous judgment.

II Samuel 10:4 (ESV)
So Hanun took David's servants and shaved off half the beard of each and cut off their garments in the middle, at their hips, and sent them away.

In that ancient culture and even still today in the Middle East, this would be a grave offense. Adding to the insult, Hanun ordered that the men's buttocks be exposed and sent them back publicly on the roads they previously traveled. It would not only be embarrassing but shameful. People conquered in battle were often led away as captives in this manner. We know from archaeology that the Assyrians marched many Hebrew captives back to Assyria naked to add shame to the insult of being conquered.

The faith lesson we can learn from this part of the story is sometimes not one followers of God like to hear. We who follow God are often insulted and shamed in front of the public. If you follow God long enough, it usually will happen to you. You may recall that Jesus was naked when he was crucified. That was the Roman way to add shame to the death. The first people to crucify victims were the Assyrians, and they too executed their victims without clothing. Just as David instructed his ambassadors to hide in Jericho until they had recovered from their shame, God holds us close while we recover from our hurts. Time does heal many things.

The rest of the story goes very badly for Hanun and the Ammonites. Realizing their mistake too late, they went to war against David. Knowing that they were no match for this powerful man of God, they hired other nations to come to their aid. As expected, they were destroyed.

Fourth, we can learn from this event that we should apologize when we insult someone. Once Hanun realized his mistake, he did not go and try to make amends with David. He piled up more trouble upon his people by making David angrier. How much better would it have been for the Ammonites if Hanun had humbled himself before David. David was a man who was known for his mercy, but Hanun tried to fix the problem himself by making other enemies of David come to his aid.

When you have erred greatly by slander or insulting someone, go to that person and humble yourself. Ask for forgiveness and pray that they will forgive you. Hanun had that opportunity and failed to use it. He would have become a greater king and man if he had followed that advice. However, he allowed his pride to get in the way. It led not only to his destruction but the death of thousands.

It was the last minutes of the school day. In my class of Biology I students were just completing a dissection lab. They were cleaning up and putting the scalpels back in the numbered bins on a back table when I noticed that one of the scalpels was missing. Just a few years before this, I had a student sneak a scalpel from my room, go to the washroom, and attempt suicide by slitting her wrists. Because of this I numbered these items carefully. Now one was missing.

I asked for the door to be closed and asked who had misplaced a scalpel. No one said much. I then told them that no one would be allowed to leave the room until the missing scalpel was recovered. Pressure was building. Soon, the bell sounded and still the scalpel was missing. After I had every student dump their belongings on their desks, I quickly examined their contents for the scalpel. I found nothing. I went ahead and dismissed them. Then one of my most trusted students came and told me she saw Nancy place the scalpel in her textbook intending to steal it.

I was very stressed that the same type of instrument that got me into trouble once before had gone missing again. This student relayed to me that Nancy had told her she was going to steal it and had done it.

I didn't take time to think about it. I went to the principal's office and told him that Nancy had stolen a scalpel out of my room. He said that he would deal with it right away.

As I drove home that night in the calmness of my country drive through a park, I tried to retrace the movements of Nancy in my class. It dawned on me that she could not have possibly taken the scalpel. I replaced the blade in hers during class and it was brand new. As I thought more about this, I realized that the scalpel that was missing was one with an older blade in it. Nancy's scalpel was back in the bin. I also recalled seeing Nancy at the bin just before I noticed the scalpel missing. I had trouble sleeping that night because I had falsely accused Nancy.

When I got to school the next morning, the principal called me to his office. He said Nancy's mother was very upset that I accused Nancy of stealing and Nancy denied stealing the scalpel. But he told me not to worry, and that he would get it back from her even if he had to expel her.

In misery, I told him, "I made a mistake. I know she could not have done this." It had to be someone else. He said that he felt very relieved as he knew Nancy well and did not believe that she would steal from me. I talked to Nancy's parent on the phone and apologized. Then I sought out Nancy at the school. To say that she hated me was an understatement. My relationship with her was damaged and, unfortunately, though she said she forgave me, I could tell she never did.

I looked back and saw that I did the same thing Hanun did. He didn't check out the facts and, under stress, I, too, made a very regrettable decision.

Fan the Flame

In this chapter we see Hanun digging himself deeper and deeper into a hole. He failed to get the facts. All he had to do was ask his father's advisors what they knew about King David. Instead, he made a decision based on gossip and rumors and humiliated the servants of David which ended up getting a strong reaction from David. This would have been a good place to stop; but no, Hanun decided to bring others into the fiasco and found himself involved in a war. Acknowledging his mistake and making a simple apology would have stopped the death of many people.

It's human nature to fight back, but it often just makes the situation worse. Take a moment to consider where you have passed on gossip when you didn't know what the actual facts were. Were there any consequences?

_____

_____

_____

_____

What about Facebook? Have you posted to a person's account anything questionable? Did you listen to your peers and accept what they said at face value? Sure, they're your friends and you should be able to trust them. But what if what they told you is something they heard but didn't verify? One rumor can start an avalanche.

What does the Bible have to say? Read Proverbs 16:28 and 26:20 and note what can happen.

_____

_____

_____

_____

Read Romans 1:28-32 and II Corinthians 12:20 and make a list of what actions/attitudes are included with those who gossip.

_____

_____

_____

_____

Be strong. Ask God to help you figure out what to do when you are confronted with a juicy piece of gossip. Remember, what you do next will have further consequences.

Baruch
How Are You at Working for God?

Years ago, when I was the head of the science department at a high school, our school hired two new teachers. One was just out of college and the other was an experienced teacher from another school. Both came into our school and struggled as many new teachers do at a new school. I was responsible to make sure that they would find their niche and help them in any way I could.

The new college graduate had some problems with her teaching and was struggling. One night she came into my room in tears. "I am such a terrible teacher!" she cried. She said that her lessons were terrible, and she was wondering if she made a mistake in coming to this school. I tried to encourage her and asked what I could do for her. She told me that the principal was coming into her classroom to observe her in a few days, and she needed some coaching with her lesson. I listened to her, and she showed me her lesson plan. I saw many errors in how she was planning to present the lesson, so I asked her if she would like to use one of my old lessons from when I taught that subject. She agreed and the next couple of evenings after school, I coached her. After a few days, she seemed ready for her observation. Finally, the day came, and the principal observed her. Afterwards, he told her that she did a fabulous job! He praised her highly in all aspects from classroom discipline to the fun way she informed the students. She quietly accepted this praise.

The next day I had a meeting with the principal about her and he told me that she was doing great. He related how impressed he was with her lesson and delivery. He told me he was pleased with our decision to hire her because she would fit in nicely at our school.

On another day, the new experienced teacher we had hired was facing a similar problem. He was just as discouraged about his teaching abilities, and he was feeling like a failure. What was worse to him was that the principal was soon coming into his room for observation. He asked me for help, so again I suggested using one of my lessons on the concept. We spent time practicing the lesson and soon he was much more confident. When the day came that the principal observed him, everything went smoothly, and he impressed our boss. After the class, the principal met with him and said that he was very impressed with the lesson and his delivery. He confessed that I had helped him and coached him on using one of my lessons. The principal could see my influence on the lesson, but he told the teacher it was fine.

When the principal and I met to discuss the performance of that teacher, he said he was impressed. I smiled, relieved by the good news. After he relayed that he knew I had helped the teacher with the lesson, I sat there wondering what he thought of my coaching. He told me he appreciated the teacher's honesty as well as my contribution in helping the staff be successful.

Often there is a behind-the-scenes person who influences others and is not recognized. Walk down the street and ask people if they have ever heard of a prophet of God named Jeremiah. Most people have and are aware that he has a book in the Bible named after him. But ask those same people if they have ever heard of a man named Baruch, and they will most likely not have a clue as to his identity. Many people might think you are referring to a movie character or some fictional person, but Baruch was an important biblical character, though we find his name rather hidden in Scripture.

Baruch can be found in only four chapters in the Bible. They are all in the Book of Jeremiah, because…well…he wrote that book. Yes, Baruch took stylus in hand and wrote the Book of Jeremiah. Jeremiah dictated what to write and Baruch wrote it. In fact, his first copy was destroyed, and he had to write another that was longer than the first edition.

Who is this little-known man who was a close friend and writer to the famous prophet Jeremiah? Why did God place him in Scripture for us to read about? What major lesson can we learn from such a seemingly insignificant fellow?

We first find Baruch in Jeremiah 32, obtaining a deed for property that Jeremiah had just bought.

Jeremiah 32:12 (KJV)
And I gave the evidence of the purchase unto Baruch the son of Neriah…and in the presence of the witnesses that subscribed the book of the purchase, before all the Jews that sat in the court of the prison.

Baruch is being introduced here as an errand boy for Jeremiah.

The next time we find Baruch in Scripture is in Jeremiah 36.

Jeremiah 36:4-8 (ESV)
Then Jeremiah called Baruch the son of Neriah, and Baruch wrote on a scroll at the dictation of Jeremiah all the words of the LORD that he had spoken to him. And Jeremiah ordered Baruch, saying, "I am banned from going to the house of the LORD, so you are to go, and on a day of fasting in the hearing of all the people in the LORD's house you shall read the words of the LORD from the scroll that you have written at my dictation. You shall read them also in the hearing of all the men of Judah who come out of their cities. It may be that their plea for mercy will come before the LORD, and that every one will turn from his evil way, for great is the anger and wrath that the LORD has pronounced against this people." And Baruch the son of Neriah did all that Jeremiah the prophet ordered him about reading from the scroll the words of the LORD in the LORD's house.

Baruch is assigned an important task to write down what Jeremiah had dictated and read it orally in the Temple. This was not going to be one of those happily-ever-after pieces of entertainment, but of terror and destruction that is about to happen to Jerusalem because of their flaunting God's Law. So, many people heard the Word of God from Baruch's lips.

Later, he was ushered in front of the palace officials and was asked to read it again in front of them.

Jeremiah 36:14-15 (ESV)
Then all the officials sent Jehudi the son of Nethaniah, son of Shelemiah, son of Cushi, to say to Baruch, "Take in your hand the scroll that you read in the hearing of the people, and come." So Baruch the son of Neriah took the scroll in his hand and came to them. And they said to him, "Sit down and read it." So Baruch read it to them.

After the reading, the officials told him to take Jeremiah and go into hiding because the king would not want to hear the message.

Jeremiah 36:19 (ESV)
Then the officials said to Baruch, "Go and hide, you and Jeremiah, and let no one know where you are."

These officials were right to tell them to hide, because King Jehoiakim of Judah did not appreciate the message from God. Observe what he did as an official named Jehudi was reading the scroll to him.

Jeremiah 36:23 (ESV)
As Jehudi read three or four columns, the king would cut them off with a knife and throw them into the fire in the fire pot, until the entire scroll was consumed in the fire that was in the fire pot.

After this scroll was burned, Jeremiah dictated another one to Baruch. Both men were undaunted by this blatant destruction of God's Word. This shows us their character. They were both totally dedicated to God and did not fear a human king. However, they did fear an awesome God.

The next mention of Baruch comes in Jeremiah 43. Here he was blamed for inciting Jeremiah against a bunch of arrogant idiots. These leaders were abusing him and lying about him.

Jeremiah 43:1-3 (ESV)
When Jeremiah finished speaking to all the people all these words of the LORD their God, with which the LORD their God had sent him to them, Azariah the son of Hoshaiah and Johanan the son of Kareah and all the insolent men said to Jeremiah, "You are telling a lie. The LORD our God did not send you to say, 'Do not go to Egypt to live there,' but Baruch the son of Neriah has set you against us, to deliver us into the hand of the Chaldeans, that they may kill us or take us into exile in Babylon."

We have one more occasion when Baruch is mentioned. Jeremiah 45, a very short chapter, is dedicated to Baruch.

Jeremiah 45:1-5 (ESV)
The word that Jeremiah the prophet spoke to Baruch the son of Neriah, when he wrote these words in a book at the dictation of Jeremiah, in the fourth year of Jehoiakim the son of Josiah, king of Judah: "Thus says the LORD, the God of Israel, to you, O Baruch: You said, 'Woe is me! For the LORD has added sorrow to my pain. I am weary with my groaning, and I find no rest.' Thus shall you say to him, Thus says the LORD: Behold, what I have built I am breaking down, and what I have planted I am plucking up—that is, the whole land. And do you seek great things for yourself? Seek them not, for behold, I am bringing disaster upon all flesh, declares the LORD. But I will give you your life as a prize of war in all places to which you may go."

Here, God both warned and promised Baruch. He told him, "Do you seek great things for yourself? Seek them not..."

What a rebuke by God! This was a man who had been in the shadow of one of the greatest prophets of all time. He had been a close friend and an assistant to Jeremiah. But God specifically warned him not to seek great things for himself. Was Baruch starting to be a bit jealous of Jeremiah and all of the fame and recognition he was getting? It appears so. Maybe that's why God placed this short little chapter in this book, to be a rebuke for any of us who seek great things for ourselves.

So how are you at working for God? Do you get a little annoyed when someone else you work with seems to get all the praise? Do you feel that you are being overlooked, even though you are working just as hard if not harder than others who are getting the credit? How are you at being in the shadow of someone else? Can you live with being in the shadows of those greater and still rejoice that they are getting the acknowledgements? If you ever felt like that, I am sure Baruch did too. God gave Baruch a specific message about those feelings. (And remember, Baruch was the one writing this down for Jeremiah. That alone must have been difficult.) But God also gave him a special gift...He said that He will give him his life as a prize.

I think that there are some great faith lessons for us from Baruch.

- He was a faithful friend, even when Jeremiah was unpopular.
- He did not desert Jeremiah when things got tough.
- He was courageous enough to place his life on the line to read a very unpopular message from God in front of the multitudes and the high officials.
- He was attacked, blamed, and lied about because of his friendship with Jeremiah.
- He was willing to stay in the shadow of a famous person to have the Word of God proclaimed.
- He was honest and proclaimed that he was just a scribe and not the author of the scroll. He could have claimed it as his own work.

We, too, must realize that God is to be honored and not us. God is to get the glory and not us. God is to be praised and not us. God is the author of anything good coming from our lives. It is not us. Baruch understood humility. Do we?

When a person becomes a Christian, Jesus determines what spiritual gift He will give a person and the Holy Spirit delivers it to them. All Christians have at least one spiritual gift. And there is not one gift that is more important than another, though to the flesh it may seem like it. Paul writes a lot about this in I Corinthians 12.

William Barclay, in his commentary *The Gospel of Luke*, records an interesting lesson about humility.

The humility of Principal Cairns was phenomenal, he is so well known in the educational world. He would never enter a room first. He would always step back and say, "No, here, you go, and I'll follow," though he was so well known and respected by the public.

On one occasion, as he stepped up to climb the steps to go to one of the seats on the platform, the public noticed who he was and immediately burst into applause. Shocked, he turned and looked and stepped back and had the man behind him go ahead. And he applauded the man who had walked up behind him, thinking the applause was for him. That isn't phony humility; that's true humility. It never dawned on him that the public would applaud him.[7]

Fan the Flame

Have you ever felt you were treated with indifference? Do you feel like you don't get the acknowledgement you deserve? In our work for God, we should never feel inferior to another Christian worker, nor should we be treated that way. Look at I Corinthians 12. It begins by talking about the gifts God has given us. Gifts we are to use for the common good. But keep reading. Take a close look at verses 14-25. What is it saying about individual Christian workers?

---

7 • Barclay, W. (1975). The Necessity of Humility (Luke 14:7-11). In *The Gospel of Luke. The Westminster Press.*

On the other hand, God also has something to say about pride. Write out the following verses.

I Peter 5:5

Proverbs 8:13

Proverbs 16:18 _____

_____

_____

_____

_____

_____

Here are a couple of things God has to say about humility:

Philippians 2:3 _____

_____

_____

_____

_____

_____

_____

I Peter 5:5 _____

_____

_____

_____

_____

_____

_____

As a Christian, we must always keep an eye on our attitude. We are all joint workers of God, neither inferior nor superior.

Balaam & Balak
Bartering With God

Some people have a great desire to hear the Word of God. Back when I was a freshman at Olivet Nazarene University, there was a guy who lived on the first floor of the freshman dorm whom we will call John. To say that John struggled as a student is an understatement, but he had a good heart. John always insisted on studying with the radio tuned to Gospel music, which his roommate could not stand. They often battled about the environment of the room when it came time to study. John had to have the music on, while his roommate had to study in absolute silence.

One night, John's roommate came up to my room where a bunch of us were just sitting and talking. He entered saying in a disgusted voice that John was at it again, studying with that music on. I asked him and the others in my room, "Do you want to pull a prank on John?" Everyone heartily agreed. I must admit, my sinful nature overtook me. What I proposed was so mean and evil...Lord, forgive me. I told them all that I had built a transmitter when I was in junior high school, and I had it in the closet. I suggested that we go into the room next door to John and talk to John through his radio. They all agreed to my evil scheme.

We entered the room next door with great enthusiasm. I sat at the transmitter while others held drink glasses to their ears and leaned against the wall separating John from us. In a few moments, I had found the frequency John was listening to, for suddenly his radio went silent. What now transpired we can only guess, for although we could not see what was in the room, we could hear what was taking place.

We let the radio remain silent for quite a few moments before one of the guys in on the prank spoke with his deep bass voice into the microphone, "John!" This was followed by a moment of silence. Then he spoke again into the microphone, "John!"

We heard John reply, "Who is that?"

Our guy said, "It's the Lord, John!"

There was a distinct pause before John called out, "Who is this really?"

Our guy said again, "It's the Lord, John! I am coming to you from this radio."

John finally replied, "Yes, Lord, I hear you. What do you want to say to me?"

Our guy said, "John, I want you to quit school tomorrow and buy a plane ticket to Uganda. There you will become my new Paul, my new Billy Graham. You will lead thousands to me in stadiums across Africa. Now go, John!"

It wasn't until this point that we all suddenly realized what a bad prank this was. It was as if the Holy Spirit instantly convicted all of us of the sin we were doing, because John started yelling and shouting out, "Yes, Lord! Yes, Lord! I will start packing now and leave tomorrow!"

We heard him crying as he was shouting. I quietly told the others in the room, "Guys, we have really done a bad thing here. We need to go in there and tell him that this was a joke. I just never really thought he would believe this."

So, we all entered John's room together and found him on his knees clutching the radio and crying.

"John," we tried to tell him, "We were just pulling a practical joke on you."

But before we could get it all out, he got up and began telling us how God actually spoke to him through the radio. We tried and tried to tell him that it was us just playing a joke on him, but he was convinced that it was truly the Lord speaking to him through his radio.

Finally, we had to get the transmitter and show him how we did this terrible act. When our guy spoke into the microphone and John heard the voice again, his joy suddenly turned to rage. We were lucky to get out of his room alive!

King Balak of Moab had a problem. The Israelites on their exodus from Egypt were invading Canaan and had just destroyed the Amorites because the Amorites did not allow the Israelites to pass through their land. So, God commanded Moses to destroy the Amorites for refusing to help the Israelites. After this victory, the Israelites camped next to the land of Moab, ruled by King Balak. Balak thought that the Israelites were going to attack him too.

Numbers 22:2-3 (ESV)
And Balak the son of Zippor saw all that Israel had done to the Amorites. And Moab was in great dread of the people, because they were many. Moab was overcome with fear of the people of Israel.

Balak and all in his kingdom were scared to death about their impending future. He knew that his army was no match for the Israelites, so he looked for help. However, he shouldn't have been worried nor frightened by this because God had told Moses not to attack Moab.

Deuteronomy 2:9 (ESV)
And the LORD said to me, "Do not harass Moab or contend with them in battle, for I will not give you any of their land for a possession, because I have given Ar to the people of Lot for a possession."

Balak was unnecessarily afraid. He had probably heard that Israel would not attack him but did not believe it. So, he sought out

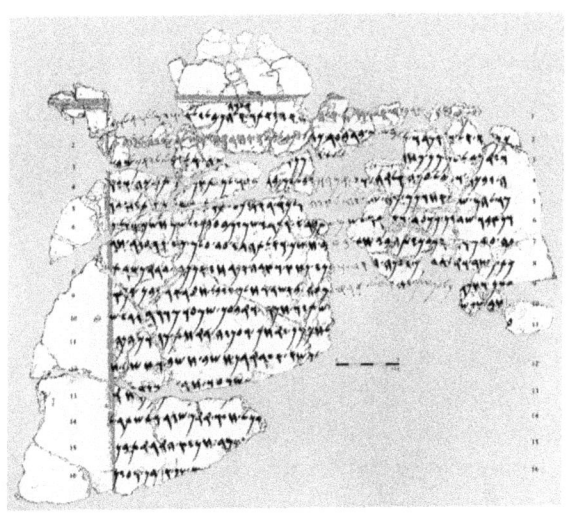

◀ Reproduction of the fragments from the Book of Balaam found at Deir Alla (Disdero / Wikimedia, CC BY SA 4.0)

One of the inscriptions reads…"[Ba]laam [son of Beo]r, the man who was a seer of the gods."

Map derived from Enyavar et al. Wikimedia, CC BY-SA 4.0
▼

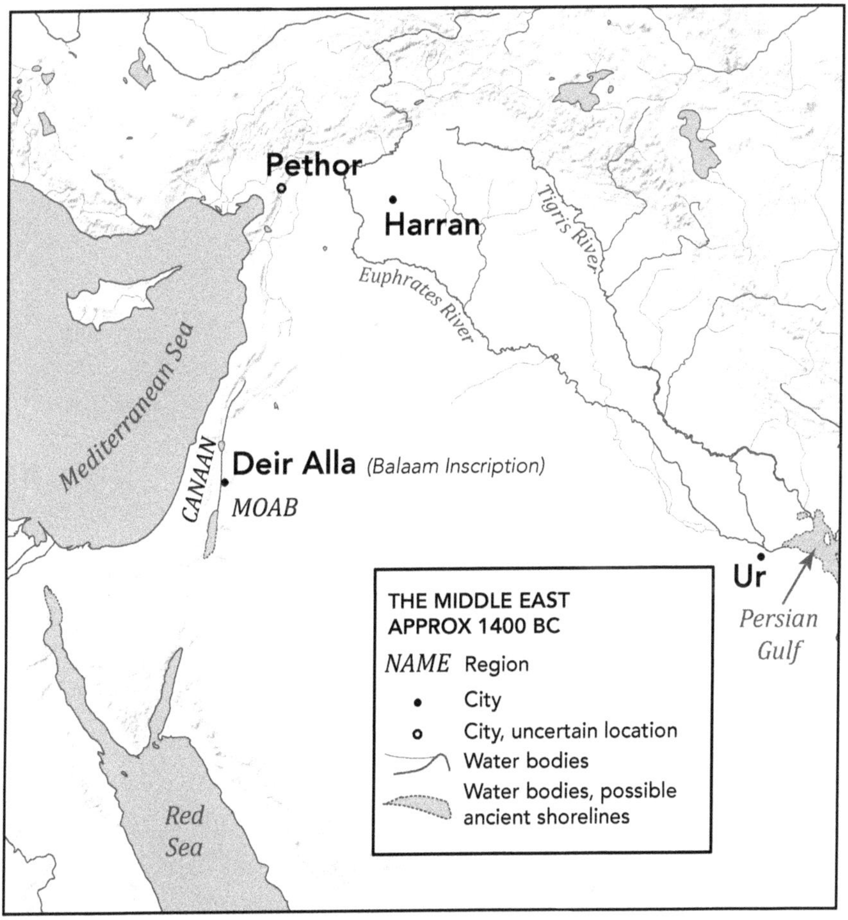

Pethor

Harran

Tigris River

Euphrates River

Mediterranean Sea

CANAAN

Deir Alla (Balaam Inscription)

MOAB

Ur

Persian Gulf

THE MIDDLE EAST
APPROX 1400 BC

NAME Region
● City
○ City, uncertain location
⌇ Water bodies
⌇ Water bodies, possible ancient shorelines

Red Sea

a plan to prevent the Israelites from conquering Moab. He did not take God's Word as truth and instead, tried to set his own agenda that was contrary to God's Word.

Numbers 22:4b-6 (ESV)

So Balak the son of Zippor, who was king of Moab at that time, sent messengers to Balaam the son of Beor at Pethor, which is near the River in the land of the people of Amaw, to call him, saying, "Behold, a people has come out of Egypt. They cover the face of the earth, and they are dwelling opposite me. Come now, curse this people for me, since they are too mighty for me. Perhaps I shall be able to defeat them and drive them from the land, for I know that he whom you bless is blessed, and he whom you curse is cursed."

Balaam was a prophet for hire. We often teach children about him and his talking donkey; but if we examine the Word of God carefully, we can get the impression that Balaam was not just a prophet of God but of many gods. He was a diviner of many pagan gods and not the great biblical hero some people make him out to be.

Numbers 22:7 (ESV)

So the elders of Moab and the elders of Midian departed with the fees for divination in their hand. And they came to Balaam and gave him Balak's message.

Balaam is referred to here as a diviner who accepted fees. No doubt he had a working knowledge of YHWH, but he most likely was compensated for consulting other gods. This was very common in ancient Canaan, and modern archaeology has found artifacts naming Balaam, Son of Beor, as a seer or diviner.

Given that Balaam lived over 400 miles away from Balak, near the city of Haran where Abraham lived, he must have had a widely known reputation in Canaan.

Now we have two characters in this study. One is Balak, who was searching for God's Word, or more specifically "God's curse" on

Israel. He was willing to go to great lengths to hear God's Word, even if it meant it would cost him and would entail sending for a messenger hundreds of miles away.

I must pause at this point to look at a faith lesson that is begging to be declared. It is this: What lengths are you willing to go to hear the Word of God? Would you give up much of your wealth to obtain it? Would you travel hundreds of miles on foot to obtain it? How much do you really and truly want to hear God speak to you?

Balak's messengers arrived at the home of Balaam where he received them, and the story continues.

Numbers 22:7-14 (ESV)
So the elders of Moab and the elders of Midian departed with the fees for divination in their hand. And they came to Balaam and gave him Balak's message. And he said to them, "Lodge here tonight, and I will bring back word to you, as the Lord speaks to me." So the princes of Moab stayed with Balaam. And God came to Balaam and said, "Who are these men with you?" And Balaam said to God, "Balak the son of Zippor, king of Moab, has sent to me, saying, 'Behold, a people has come out of Egypt, and it covers the face of the earth. Now come, curse them for me. Perhaps I shall be able to fight against them and drive them out." God said to Balaam, "You shall not go with them. You shall not curse the people, for they are blessed." So Balaam rose in the morning and said to the princes of Balak, "Go to your own land, for the LORD has refused to let me go with you." So the princes of Moab rose and went to Balak and said, "Balaam refuses to come with us."

Balaam did as he should and waited to hear from God on His will in this matter. As has been stated already, Balaam was a seer of the gods, but he knew about YHWH too. So, he waited to hear, and God responded by telling him not to curse the people nor even to go with them. Balaam at this point did what was right. He listened for God's Word. When he received it, he followed it.

Let us pause to see a faith lesson here that we can implement in our lives. When Balaam was searching for God's Word on the subject, he got his answer. God was blunt and to the point. There could be no doubt in Balaam's mind as to God's wishes on the matter of these Israelites. After receiving God's Word during the night, Balaam rose first thing in the morning and told his guests to leave. He did not wait around hoping for payment or some clause that could be added to the case. He simply told them, "Go to your own land, for the Lord has refused to let me go with you." How many times do we seek God's will in a circumstance, hear it plainly, and then doubt or try to reason with God because we did not like His answer. Balaam at this point in our lesson has done what is right. No doubt he probably wished he could go, get paid, and receive some good PR for free. But he did what God told him to do.

On the other hand, Balak has not learned the lesson that Balaam has. Observe how he responded to the answer he received from God.

Numbers 22:15-17 (ESV)
Once again Balak sent princes, more in number and
more honorable than these. And they came to Balaam
and said to him, "Thus says Balak the son of Zippor:
'Let nothing hinder you from coming to me, for I will
surely do you great honor, and whatever you say to
me I will do. Come, curse this people for me.'"

Isn't this like many people today? They seek God's Word for their life, but when God "disappoints" them by not agreeing with their requests, they try to reason with God and get Him to see it from their point of view. How simplified and better their lives would be if they simply accepted God's Word and ran with it.

Balak, not happy with the response he received, tried once more. Balaam again received Balak's messengers. Notice that the message these men handed to Balaam was one promising great honor and wealth. But look how Balaam handled this entourage of guests and their promises.

Numbers 22:18-21 (ESV)
But Balaam answered and said to the servants of Balak,
"Though Balak were to give me his house full of silver
and gold, I could not go beyond the command of the LORD
my God to do less or more. So you, too, please stay here
tonight, that I may know what more the LORD will say to
me." And God came to Balaam at night and said to him,
"If the men have come to call you, rise, go with them; but
only do what I tell you." So Balaam rose in the morning and
saddled his donkey and went with the princes of Moab.

Why did Balaam invite them in and intercede for them for the Lord? He already knew God's feeling toward this matter. The reason he does this is explained in other places in the Bible.

II Peter 2:15 (ESV)
Forsaking the right way, they have gone astray.
They have followed the way of Balaam, the son
of Beor, who loved gain from wrongdoing...

Jude 1:11 (ESV)
Woe to them! For they walked in the way of Cain
and abandoned themselves for the sake of gain to
Balaam's error and perished in Korah's rebellion.

Balaam had a greater love of materialistic things and money than he had for God. He had already asked God for guidance on this matter and God responded to him. When weeks later he was readdressed by Balak, he was tempted to see if God would allow him to garner fame and wealth.

When you are trying to find out God's will for your life and He responds in a way that is clear but not favorable to you, do you try to bargain with Him or get Him to compromise or change His mind? That is what Balaam was attempting here. He already knew what God wanted, but he was determined to try His patience. This, of course, angered God to the point that He set out to kill Balaam. This is the famous story of Balaam and his talking donkey. The donkey saw the angel of the Lord standing in the road with a sword. The donkey saved Balaam's life, but not before he beat the donkey with his staff. Then God opened the eyes of Balaam and told him that the donkey saved his life.

Numbers 22:34-35 (ESV)
Then Balaam said to the angel of the Lord, "I have sinned, for I did not know that you stood in the road against me. Now therefore, if it is evil in your sight, I will turn back." And the angel of the Lord said to Balaam, "Go with the men, but speak only the word that I tell you." So Balaam went on with the princes of Balak.

Balaam had the wrong motives in serving Balak. He was not as concerned about serving God as he was about getting fame and wealth. Because of this, God almost killed him.

There are times when we will deliberately disobey God for our personal reasons. But God is sovereign and is not thwarted by our disobedience. He knows what we are going to do before we do it and has a plan ready for when we disobey. How easier and more abundant our lives would be if we just accepted and obeyed God's Word instead of trying to manipulate God into our way of thinking.

Balaam finally arrived in Moab, and Balak was there to meet him. He asked Balaam to curse the Israelites at Bamoth-Baal (Mount Baal). But instead of a curse, Balaam pronounced a great blessing on the Israelites.

Balak was beside himself with horror and declared...

Numbers 23:11-12 (ESV)
And Balak said to Balaam, "What have you done to me? I took you to curse my enemies, and behold, you have done nothing but bless them." And he answered and said, "Must I not take care to speak what the Lord puts in my mouth?"

Balaam gave Balak the right answer again. He said that he must only speak what God has willed. But Balak was undeterred with

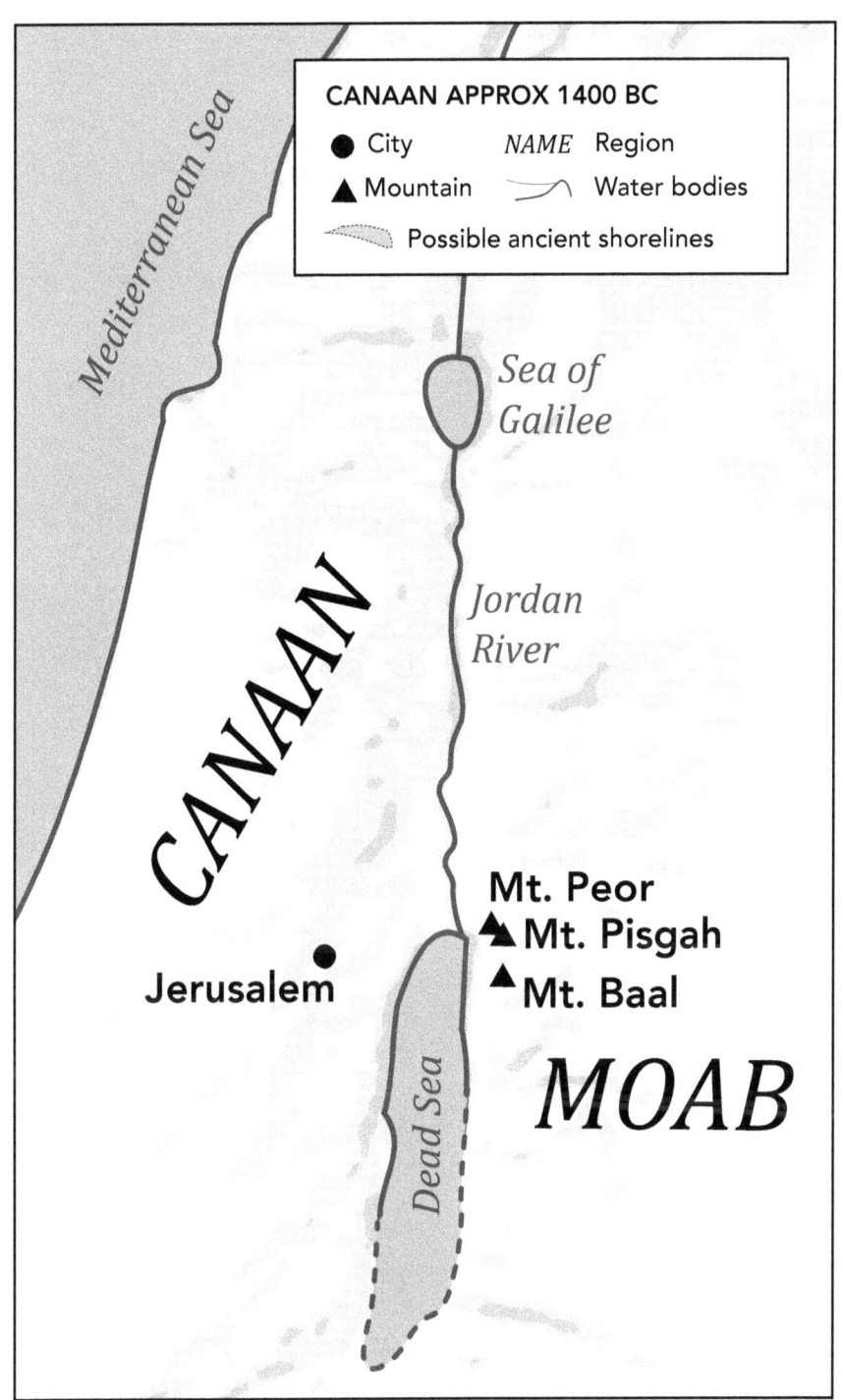

CANAAN APPROX 1400 BC
- ● City
- ▲ Mountain
- *NAME* Region
- 〜 Water bodies
- 〜 Possible ancient shorelines

Mediterranean Sea

Sea of Galilee

Jordan River

CANAAN

Mt. Peor
▲ Mt. Pisgah
▲ Mt. Baal

Jerusalem ●

Dead Sea

MOAB

Map derived from World Search Bible, Natural Earth (Wikimedia) / CC BY-SA 4.0, & Enyavar et al. (Wikimedia) / CC BY-SA 4.0, this event as he pressed Balaam to pronounce a curse from a different location on a partial group of Israelites.

Numbers 23:13-14 (ESV)
And Balak said to him, "Please come with me to another place, from which you may see them. You shall see only a fraction of them and shall not see them all. Then curse them for me from there." And he took him to the field of Zophim, to the top of Pisgah.

Once again Balaam got it right and pronounced a blessing on the Israelites and not a curse.

Numbers 23:25-28 (ESV)
And Balak said to Balaam, "Do not curse them at all, and do not bless them at all." But Balaam answered Balak, "Did I not tell you, 'All that the Lord says, that I must do'?" And Balak said to Balaam, "Come now, I will take you to another place. Perhaps it will please God that you may curse them for me from there." So Balak took Balaam to the top of Peor, which overlooks the desert.

Here we go again. Balak tried to manipulate God again, but it didn't work. Three times Balak tried God's patience and all three times he received the same answer. Now Balak was really mad.

Numbers 24:10-11 (ESV)
And Balak's anger was kindled against Balaam, and he struck his hands together. And Balak said to Balaam, "I called you to curse my enemies, and behold, you have blessed them these three times. Therefore now flee to your own place. I said, 'I will certainly honor you,' but the Lord has held you back from honor."

Another faith lesson faces us from Balak's actions. He tried to find out God's will in his life. He asked God and God replied. But he was not happy with God's plan, so he tried to manipulate God into making a favorable reply. Three times he badgered God, slightly altering his request each time. But God is not man that He changes His mind.

Numbers 23:19 (ESV)
God is not man, that he should lie, or a son of man, that he should change his mind. Has he said, and will he not do it? Or has he spoken, and will he not fulfill it?

Balak had to learn this the hard way; and today, people are still trying to learn this. Many Christians think they can justify their sins by reasoning that God will accept whatever they do, even if it is contrary to His Word, because He wants them to be happy. I tell you this in all earnestness: God does not change His mind, especially in areas of sin. Because God is holy, sin cannot be a part of Him. He calls us to be holy too.

I Peter 1:14-16 (ESV)
As obedient children, do not be conformed to the passions of your former ignorance, but as he who called you is holy, you also be holy in all your conduct, since it is written, "You shall be holy, for I am holy."

One more point should be made concerning Balaam, and it deals with his discourses. There is one discourse that is very special. Let's examine it.

Numbers 24:17-19 (ESV)
I behold him, but not near: a star shall come out of Jacob, and a scepter shall rise out of Israel; it shall crush the forehead of Moab and break down all the sons of Sheth. Edom shall be dispossessed; Seir also, his enemies, shall be dispossessed. Israel is doing valiantly. And one from Jacob shall exercise dominion and destroy the survivors of cities!"

This passage is Balaam's fourth oracle. He was prophesying under the influence of God concerning the blessing of Israel. There are key references being made here concerning the future King David and also the Messiah. David, of course, was victorious in battle over Moab and Edom. But as with many messianic prophecies, David is but a forerunner of a future fulfillment performed by the Messiah. In this oracle or discourse of Balaam, we see three key prophecies concerning the Messiah.

1. He was not to arise in the near future. (Historians view this to be written around 1407 BC.) The "not now" found in verse 17 makes this very clear. In fact, he would not appear until after other nations have come and gone, which are mentioned in verses 20-24. In verse 24, one nation, Kittim, is listed. Kittim is a reference to the Greek empire. So, the Messiah would come after the Greek empire, which of course is exactly what happened.

2. He is to be like a star. In Revelation 22:16, Jesus refers to Himself as "the bright Morning Star."

Revelation 22:16 (ESV)
"I, Jesus, have sent my angel to testify to you about these things for the churches. I am the root and the descendant of David, the bright Morning Star."

Jesus is the light of salvation to all fallen men. Some theologians believe that this might be a passage that the Magi used to locate the Messiah in Matthew's Gospel. It is quite probable that the Magi had access to this passage, though some discount this because Matthew did not use it as a reference in his Gospel as he usually does with other prophecies.

3. He will be mighty. He will be victorious over His enemies. "He will crush" His enemies. Jesus came after Moab was completely destroyed and the Romans were destroying the last remnants of Edom when Jesus was born.

Now we have another faith lesson. Even though God was not overly pleased with Balaam's sinful and selfish ambitions, God did use him to proclaim an important prophecy concerning King David and Jesus. This shows us that even people who are evil and not walking close with God can still be used by Him. Balaam would eventually be killed by the Israelites because of his evil influence. Some people think that because they perform tasks for God and work for Him, He will pardon their sins. But that is not the case. Recall what Jesus said about such people.

Matthew 7:21-23 (ESV)
"Not everyone who says to me, 'Lord, Lord,' will enter the

kingdom of heaven, but the one who does the will of my Father who is in heaven. On that day many will say to me, 'Lord, Lord, did we not prophesy in your name, and cast out demons in your name, and do many mighty works in your name?' And then will I declare to them, 'I never knew you; depart from me, you workers of lawlessness.'"

This passage should make some people reexamine their lives and their motives as they work for God. Balaam was not a true follower of God and was condemned by many writers of the New Testament. Yet he seemed to be working for God. He even prophesied in His name about David and Jesus, but he never really knew God. How about you? Do you think that by working for God in church, at a Christian camp, or another such place, it makes you a follower of Jesus?

It now appears that we are near the end of the story of Balaam and Balak in Numbers because we read that Balaam and Balak separated.

Numbers 24:25 (ESV)
Then Balaam rose and went back to his place. And Balak also went his way.

But that is not the case! We find out later that before Balaam left and went home, he gave a suggestion to Balak about how to counter God's blessings on Israel. Can you believe what Balaam was doing here? No doubt, he did this to win the fame and wealth that Balak had promised him. The clue is found in chapter 31 of Numbers and in the book of Revelation.

Numbers 31:16 (ESV)
Behold, these, on Balaam's advice, caused the people of Israel to act treacherously against the Lord in the incident of Peor, and so the plague came among the congregation of the Lord.

Revelation 2:14 (ESV)
But I have a few things against you: you have some there who hold the teaching of Balaam, who taught Balak to put a stumbling block before the sons of Israel, so that they might eat food sacrificed to idols and practice sexual immorality.

It appears that Balaam, wanting fame and wealth, was not such a good prophet of God as we are often led to believe. True, he did not curse Israel, but he told Balak that if the Moabite women engaged in sexual acts with the Israelite men and got the men to eat food sacrificed to idols, that God would punish them and kill many of them. That was precisely what happened.

What can we learn from these two characters? I think five things stand out. First, how far are you willing to go to hear God's Word? Second, it is good to seek God's Word in trying to find out your future. Third, when seeking out God's Word, listen to Him and accept it. Don't doubt His response to you. Fourth, do not try to manipulate or barter with God. He does not change. So do not try God's patience. If you don't like His answer, don't keep making conditions until you think He will relent and allow you to do what you want. Fifth, and this one is very important, just because you say you worship God and do work for Him doesn't mean that you are walking close with God or really know Him.

There was a girl who was president of her high school student council. She was also extremely active in her church's youth group where she was vice president. She often sang specials in the morning church services and loved to talk about how after college she planned to go to Africa and be a missionary/nurse. She seemed to have it all together. She loved to lead worship and work for God. It appeared to all of us that she was walking close with God. But she had a secret. Although she had a boyfriend who was also walking with God, she was having a sexual affair with one of her teachers at her high school. This had been going on for a couple of years, but her boyfriend found out in his senior year. He came to me and asked for help about what to do. I went to her and asked what in the world she was thinking. She replied that at first, she thought it was wrong, but because she loved him and he told her he loved her, this was not against God's will. She asked me, "If this is so wrong, why does it feel so right?"

I could not believe that this was the same girl I had known. She told me that it started out innocently, but they both began to have a great desire and love for each other. And besides that, she was witnessing to him and maybe this relationship would be used by God to bring him to a saving knowledge of Jesus Christ.

I could not believe what I was hearing. She was trying to manipulate God into accepting this relationship and sin into some kind of evangelism to honor God. She went on to try to explain to me how God could use this situation to bring glory to Himself. And she finished by telling me that God is a God of love and would not want her to be unhappy; therefore, He was accepting this. Besides, it had been going on for a long time and she was still doing great work for Him in the church. I just thought how true Jesus' words are...

Matthew 7:21-23 (ESV)
"Not everyone who says to me, 'Lord, Lord,' will enter the kingdom of heaven, but the one who does the will of my Father who is in heaven. On that day many will say to me, 'Lord, Lord, did we not prophesy in your name, and cast out demons in your name, and do many mighty works in your name?' And then will I declare to them, 'I never knew you; depart from me, you workers of lawlessness.'"

Fan the Flame

Today's technology makes it much easier to hear/read God's Word. If you want an answer from God, how would you go about getting it?

If you received an answer from God, did you accept it? Did anyone try to change your mind perhaps by giving what sounded like a good reason? Did you "hang tight" or did you keep asking God to reconsider based on what you learned? Take some time to consider what your response has been to such situations. Do you need to adjust your thinking, or have you kept true to what God told you?

Did you catch the situation between Balaam and God? God eventually tells Balaam to go ahead and go to Moab, but He obviously was angry about the situation. Enough so that an angel of God intended to kill him on his journey rather than allow him to curse God's people. Why did God "change" His mind? God created us with a free will. It is completely up to us to obey or disobey God. We are not puppets, but human beings created in God's image (Genesis 1:27). God doesn't lead us around, manipulate us into doing what He wants. It is our choice. But our choices can anger God as it did with Balaam. When we sin, we still suffer the consequences of that sin. Look up II Samuel 11 and 12, the story of King David and Bathsheba. Although David asked for and was granted God's forgiveness, he still suffered the consequences of his sin.

Have you ever had a situation in which you believed God changed His mind? Did anything happen afterwards that should have been a warning that you were headed in the wrong direction?

Write down Numbers 23:19.

Dathan, Abiram, & Korah

Shallow Faith That Gets Swallowed Up by Doubts

Numbers 16

I once heard Chuck Swindoll tell a story about a man who had trouble believing. In the story a man from Long Island purchased a barometer one day from a well-respected company, Abercrombie & Fitch. When he brought it home and took it out of the box, he was disturbed that the needle would only point to the sector marked Hurricane. He tried shaking the delicate instrument several times (not a good idea when holding an expensive and sensitive instrument), but to no avail – it continued to point to the same sector. Frustrated and livid, he decided to write a malicious letter to the company and on the following morning, mailed it. That evening when he returned home not only was the barometer gone but also his house! The needle of that barometer had been pointing true. The month was September; the year was 1938, the day of the terrible hurricane that nearly destroyed Long Island.[8]

---

8 • Adapted from a story heard on the radio series *Insight for Living*.and Swindoll, C. R. (1998). Bible-Influence Of. In *Swindoll's Ultimate book of illustrations & quotes: Over 1,500 outstanding ways to effectively drive home your message* (pp. 50–51). T. Nelson.

My dad used to say that some people are like owls; the more light you shine on them, the blinder they become. Sometimes people are blessed to see something miraculous or experience the extraordinary and it builds up their faith. But afterwards, when the evidence is no longer visible, they doubt what they saw and fail to believe. Such was the case for three men—Dathan, Abiram, and Korah and their families.

Numbers 16:1-3 (ESV)

Now Korah the son of Izhar, son of Kohath, son of Levi, and Dathan and Abiram the sons of Eliab, and On the son of Peleth, sons of Reuben, took men. And they rose up before Moses, with a number of the people of Israel, 250 chiefs of the congregation, chosen from the assembly, well-known men. They assembled themselves together against Moses and against Aaron and said to them, "You have gone too far! For all in the congregation are holy, every one of them, and the LORD is among them. Why then do you exalt yourselves above the assembly of the LORD?"

Who are these three people?

1. Korah was a cousin of Aaron and Moses. A Levite, but not a priest. The historian Josephus tell us:

    Corah, a Hebrew of principal account both by his family and by his wealth, one that was also able to speak well, and one that could easily persuade the people by his speeches, saw that Moses was in an exceeding great dignity, and was uneasy at it, and envied him on that account (he was of the same tribe with Moses, and of kin to him), was particularly grieved, because he thought he better deserved that honorable post on account of his great riches, and not inferior to him in his birth.[9]

2. Dathan was the brother of Abiram. They were Reubenites and leaders of the tribe. They were also very wealthy.

---

9 • Josephus, Flavius, and Whiston, William (1737). Anitquities of the Jews - Book IV Ch 2 par 2. In *The Genuine Works of Flavius Josephus the Jewish Historian.*

There was a rebellion in the camp. Korah (Corah) was the ringleader. He was of the opinion that Moses was not greater than any other Israelite, and that he, because of his great wealth and social status, should be the leader. But why were Dathan and Abiram involved in this sedition? There are two reasons why. Reuben was the first born of Jacob and the birthright would have passed to him and his descendants. The reason Reuben was not the leading tribe was because Jacob told him he would not be. He did not get the birthright, Judah did. Why? Reuben slept with Jacob's wife Bilhah, his stepmother.

Genesis 49:3-4 (ESV)
Reuben, you are my firstborn, my might, and the firstfruits of my strength, preeminent in dignity and preeminent in power. Unstable as water, you shall not have preeminence, because you went up to your father's bed; then you defiled it—he went up to my couch!

Genesis 35:22 (ESV)
While Israel lived in that land, Reuben went and lay with Bilhah his father's concubine. And Israel heard of it.

In this ancient culture, to sleep with someone's wife was to lay claim to the position of the husband and titles. Though fueled by lust, this was more significant than just scruples. Because of his sin, he lost the birthright.

Dathan and Abiram were the tribal leaders thus, they thought Dathan should be the leader and not Moses who was born from the descendants of Levi. Besides, Dathan & Abiram were two of the wealthiest Israelites. Wealth often equals power in society.

How did Moses respond to this mutiny?

Numbers 16:4-7 (ESV)
When Moses heard it, he fell on his face, and he said to Korah and all his company, "In the morning the LORD will show who is his, and who is holy, and will bring him near to him. The one whom he chooses he will bring near to him. Do this: take censers, Korah and all his company;

*put fire in them and put incense on them before the L*ORD
*tomorrow, and the man whom the L*ORD *chooses shall
be the holy one. You have gone too far, sons of Levi!"*

What is a censer? In the days of the Tabernacle, it was a vessel used to burn incense, a privilege exclusive of the priests, the sons of Aaron. Failure to use it correctly would result in God's wrath and possibly death.

Moses challenged Korah to put fire in a censer the next day and see if God would approve of who was using it. Then Moses turned his attention to Dathan and Abiram.

Numbers 16:12-14 (ESV)
*And Moses sent to call Dathan and Abiram the sons of Eliab,
and they said, "We will not come up. Is it a small thing
that you have brought us up out of a land flowing with
milk and honey, to kill us in the wilderness, that you must
also make yourself a prince over us? Moreover, you have
not brought us into a land flowing with milk and honey,
nor given us inheritance of fields and vineyards. Will you
put out the eyes of these men? We will not come up."*

They openly defied Moses in front of the people, so Moses appealed to the Lord.

Number 16:15 (ESV)
*And Moses was very angry and said to the L*ORD*, "Do
not respect their offering. I have not taken one donkey
from them, and I have not harmed one of them."*

With the challenge set, the contest began.

Number 16:18-19 (ESV)
*So every man took his censer and put fire in them
and laid incense on them and stood at the entrance
of the tent of meeting with Moses and Aaron. Then
Korah assembled all the congregation against them
at the entrance of the tent of meeting. And the glory
of the L*ORD *appeared to all the congregation.*

The people assembled and the Lord Himself spoke:

Number 16:20-21 (ESV)
*And the L*ORD *spoke to Moses and to Aaron, saying,*
"Separate yourselves from among this congregation,
that I may consume them in a moment."

Moses saw what God was going to do and he shouted out to the people to run away and escape from the mutinous hoard.

Number 16:25-26 (ESV)
Then Moses rose and went to Dathan and Abiram,
and the elders of Israel followed him. And he spoke
to the congregation, saying, "Depart, please, from
the tents of these wicked men, and touch nothing of
theirs, lest you be swept away with all their sins."

Moses made a final speech to the people:

Number 16:28-30 (ESV)
*And Moses said, "Hereby you shall know that the L*ORD *has*
sent me to do all these works, and that it has not been of
my own accord. If these men die as all men die, or if they
*are visited by the fate of all mankind, then the L*ORD *has not*
*sent me. But if the L*ORD *creates something new, and the*
ground opens its mouth and swallows them up with all that
belongs to them, and they go down alive into Sheol, then
*you shall know that these men have despised the L*ORD*."*

Moses declared that if these people die a natural death, Korah was correct. But if the mutinous rebels die an unusual death, God had chosen.

Numbers 16:31-35 (ESV)
And as soon as he had finished speaking all these words,
the ground under them split apart. And the earth opened its
mouth and swallowed them up, with their households and all
the people who belonged to Korah and all their goods. So they
and all that belonged to them went down alive into Sheol,
and the earth closed over them, and they perished
from the midst of the assembly. And all Israel

who were around them fled at their cry, for they said,
"Lest the earth swallow us up!" And fire came out from the
LORD and consumed the 250 men offering the incense.

The lesson here is simple. Think about all of the things that these three people and the 250 other dissidents had observed since Moses began his ministry. At the hand of Moses, they had witnessed the following miracles:

- Plague of blood (Exodus 7:14-24)
- Plague of frogs (Exodus 7:25-8:15)
- Plague of gnats (Exodus 8:16-19)
- Plague of flies (Exodus 8:20-32)
- Plague against livestock (Exodus 9:1-7)
- Plague of boils (Exodus 9:8-12)
- Plague of hail (Exodus 9:13-35)
- Plague of locusts (Exodus 10:1-20)
- Plague of darkness (Exodus 10:21-29)
- Plague of death to firstborn (Exodus 11-12:32)
- Fire by night to lead the way (Exodus 13:21)
- Cloud by day to lead the way (Exodus 13:21)
- Pillar of fire to stop the Egyptians (Exodus 14:19-20)
- Crossing the Red Sea (Exodus 14:21-31)
- Healing the waters at Marah (Exodus 15:22-26)
- Coming of the quail (Exodus 16:11-13a)
- Manna from Heaven (Exodus 16: 12-19)
- Water from the Rock (Exodus 17:1-7)
- Victory over the Amalekites (Exodus 17:8-16)
- Hearing God speak to Moses at Mt. Sinai (Exodus 19:20-chapter 20)
- The radiant face of Moses when he met with God (Exodus 34:29-35)

Considering being witnesses to these miracles at his hand, Moses had quite a resume to demonstrate that he was God's chosen leader. We see that the people had not only rebelled against Moses, but against God.

Numbers 16:11 (ESV)
Therefore it is against the L<small>ORD</small> that you and all your company have gathered together.

There is a major lesson Christians can learn from this. Sometimes people who work in ministry fall into the same trap. They have seen what God has done in the lives of people; but after a period of time, they feel that they are not in need of God. They usually display certain conditions when this happens.

1. Their prayer life dwindles. They fail to spend quality time with God in prayer.
2. Their Bible study time dwindles. They fail to spend quality time in His Word.
3. They fail to spend time at church with other Christians who are walking with God and can hold them accountable.
4. They have a tendency to yield to Satan's temptations without fighting with the armor of God. Sins of lust, pride, and lying overtake them.

Korah, Dathan, and Abiram were witnesses to some of the most amazing miracles God ever conducted. They saw firsthand these incredible events. But as the time in the desert went on, they fell away from God. They allowed pride to set in. They doubted God's leadership. They refused to let God have control in their lives. They became self-centered and succumbed to their own guilty pleasures and temptations.

This falling away allows people to think that God is not that important or that His commands are not necessary. Their faith is so weak that Satan easily comes in and feasts upon them, devouring them with savor.

Back in the later 1980s and through the '90s there were many great performers in the Christian music genre. Names like Carman, Steve Green, Michael W. Smith, and others. One of the most popular was award winner Ray Boltz. He had hits with *"Thank You," "Watch the Lamb," "The Anchor Holds," "I Will Praise the Lord," "I Pledge Allegiance to the Lamb," "Feel the Nails,"* and more.

Ray Boltz was one of the top Christian artists and held concerts all over the country. He led many people to a saving knowledge of Jesus Christ. But in doing these concerts and serving in this ministry, he began to get depressed and seldom attended church with fellow believers. His devotional time with Jesus began to dwindle, and his wife noticed changes in him and in his health. The day after Christmas in 2004, he told his wife that he was gay and soon left her and his children, moving to Fort Lauderdale with his husband who was also his agent.

Ray is not the only one to fall. Many others have left the truth of God's Word and faith and are now professing atheists, universalists, or have even joined anti-Christian organizations.

We followers of Jesus need to stay close to our Father and allow the Holy Spirit to help us grow in Christ, not to be pruned from Him.

Fan the Flame

Have you ever felt that you should be the leader of a group when you aren't? Jot down the reasons for why you think this.

Now comes the hard part. Find someone who will be completely honest with you and ask him/her what they see as the reason(s) for you not being the leader. Perhaps some reasons could be "it is not your gift" or "someone else is better prepared than you" or "you need more training first" or even "people don't feel you would make a good leader." Get specifics. Talk about it with him/her and with God.

The most important thing you can do is not shy away from God. The situation may have left you angry, resentful, or even sad and depressed. Open up yourself to God and tell Him how you feel. He'll listen. Ask Him for advice and really listen to what He says. Don't keep Him out of the loop. Find someone to pray about the situation on your behalf and talk with him/her frequently.

God has provided us with wonderful teaching on how to live in harmony with others and please God. Read Romans 12. Jot down anything you feel you need to work on and anything special to you. This is a great chapter to copy and keep in a spot where you see it often. It will help you through many difficult situations.

The Prophet Who Went to Ahab
Wearing Disguises

I Kings 20:35-43

Halloween is the time of year for deception and harmless pranks. I recall back when I was in middle school one Halloween that I took advantage of wearing disguises.

My best friend David and I planned on going trick-or-treating and to do it a bit differently this time. We both remembered a few houses the year before that gave away special treats like money, extra-large candy bars, and other such things that were out of the ordinary. We decided that this year we would "hit" these houses more than once. In the past we tried it, but the homeowners would recognize our costumes and refuse us a second handout. This year, we planned to carry with us three additional costumes to change into when we discovered "special" treats at certain homes.

It all worked perfectly. When we found a house giving away $1 bills, we simply went around the side of the house and changed into another costume. Then we would reappear at the door for a second handout. Fooling the homeowners, we then went back to the side of the house and changed for another round of treats.

On this one Halloween, we did this repeatedly and never were caught. We made a real haul that night.

We sometimes encounter people who are disguised so well that we are totally taken in by them. Some know the right terms and vocabulary to use to promote their deception and dress the part very well. In drama and theater productions, disguises help set the mood and scene while making it all seem real. I myself have been involved in scores of productions and know that wearing a disguise can really help "sell the play" to the audience. I have masqueraded as the Lion in the Wizard of Oz where my wife Denise and I designed the costume complete with a movable tail. I have also masqueraded as a pirate, a town drunk, a sheriff, a detective, a Santa Claus, a butler, a chef, a prince, a soldier, a host of biblical characters, and much more. Never once did I try to pass myself off to people in town or where I work as one of those characters, with the exception of the pirate. What's more, no one ever assumed I was really a lion, a butler, Joseph, or a Roman soldier. Part of the reason for this is that I would take the mask off when the performance was over. Then the people could see the real me.

There are many Bible stories about characters wearing masks. In two of these stories, we are introduced to the masked characters, King Ahab and a prophet named Micaiah.

I Kings 20:35-43 (ESV)
And a certain man of the sons of the prophets said to his fellow at the command of the Lord, "Strike me, please." But the man refused to strike him. Then he said to him, "Because you have not obeyed the voice of the Lord, behold, as soon as you have gone from me, a lion shall strike you down." And as soon as he had departed from him, a lion met him and struck him down. Then he found another man and said, "Strike me, please." And the man struck him—struck him and wounded him. So the prophet departed and waited for the king by the way, disguising himself with a bandage over his eyes. And as the king passed, he cried to the king and said, "Your servant went out into the midst of the battle, and behold, a

soldier turned and brought a man to me and said, 'Guard this man; if by any means he is missing, your life shall be for his life, or else you shall pay a talent of silver.' And as your servant was busy here and there, he was gone." The king of Israel said to him, "So shall your judgment be; you yourself have decided it." Then he hurried to take the bandage away from his eyes, and the king of Israel recognized him as one of the prophets. And he said to him, "Thus says the LORD, 'Because you have let go out of your hand the man whom I had devoted to destruction, therefore your life shall be for his life, and your people for his people.'" And the king of Israel went to his house vexed and sullen and came to Samaria.

This story begins earlier in the chapter when King Ben-Hadad of Aram (Syria) invaded Israel. God's prophets alerted King Ahab of this military venture and over the course of a few battles, Ahab defeated and captured Ben-Hadad. According to God, Ahab was to kill Ben-Hadad but instead spared his life and signed a treaty with him. (A treaty that Ben-Hadad would break.) Ahab spared Ben-Hadad to secure a buffer nation between Israel and the new upcoming world power, Assyria. So, he neglected God's command and set up a political ally to the northeast. Ahab had accomplished the destruction of the Armenian army as God commanded, but he refused to follow **ALL** of His commands. He spared the life of the enemy king.

God's response to Ahab's disobedience was to have one of His prophets disguise himself as a wounded, common soldier who pleads for the king to hear his case and have clemency. Ahab listened to him (with Ben-Hadad present in his own chariot), and pronounced judgment, not mercy. He condemned the disguised prophet, who proceeded to remove his disguise, revealing who he really was. He then proclaimed what God has in store for Ahab.

This is often the part of the story that gets the attention but look carefully at the beginning of this passage.

And a certain man of the sons of the prophets said to his fellow at the command of the LORD, "Strike me, please."

But the man refused to strike him. Then he said to him,
"Because you have not obeyed the voice of the LORD, behold,
as soon as you have gone from me, a lion shall strike
you down." And as soon as he had departed from him,
a lion met him and struck him down.

The prophet is unidentified in the Bible, but the Jewish historian Josephus names him as Micaiah.

But a certain prophet, whose name was Micaiah, came to
one of the Israelites, and bade him smite him on the head,
for by so doing he would please God; but when he would
not do so, he foretold to him, that since he disobeyed the
commands of God, he should meet with a lion and be de-
stroyed by him.[10]

The prophet told his friend and companion to strike him with a sword. The friend refused to do this. This was a direct violation of God's Word. As a result, he paid for it with his life! If God killed the "good" man and friend of Micaiah for disobeying His Word, how much more would God punish evil Ahab for disobeying?

Micaiah then turned to a bystander and told him to smite him in obedience to God.

Then he found another man and said, "Strike me, please."
And the man struck him—struck him and wounded him.

Again, looking to the works of Josephus, the historian tells us that Micaiah was struck in the head, thus making the bandage cover his face to deceive Ahab. And the trick worked, for Ahab did not recognize Micaiah.

The prophet then told the king of the curse of God that was on him now.

And he said to him, "Thus says the LORD, 'Because
you have let go out of your hand the man whom I

---

10 • Josephus, Flavius, and Whiston, William (1737). Anitquities of the Jews - Book VIII Ch 14 par 5. In *The Genuine Works of Flavius Josephus the Jewish Historian.*

had devoted to destruction, therefore your life shall
be for his life, and your people for his people.'"

Ahab's response to this was not to seek repentance as David did when he disobeyed God. David was actually remorseful and regretted what he did. Again, Josephus records Ahab's response:

> *Upon which Ahab was very angry at the prophet, and gave commandment that he should be put in prison, and there kept* [11]

Micaiah was imprisoned for his obedience to God. This event occurred around 900 B.C. Ahab would soon be killed in battle as Elijah and Micaiah had prophesized in 897 B.C. Even in Ahab's death, a disguise was utilized, and Micaiah was back on the scene.

I Kings 22:1-8 (ESV)
For three years Syria and Israel continued without war.
But in the third year Jehoshaphat the king of Judah came
down to the king of Israel. And the king of Israel said to his
servants, "Do you know that Ramoth-gilead belongs to us,
and we keep quiet and do not take it out of the hand of the
king of Syria?" And he said to Jehoshaphat, "Will you go
with me to battle at Ramoth-gilead?" And Jehoshaphat said
to the king of Israel, "I am as you are, my people as your
people, my horses as your horses." And Jehoshaphat said to
the king of Israel, "Inquire first for the word of the LORD."
Then the king of Israel gathered the prophets together, about
four hundred men, and said to them, "Shall I go to battle
against Ramoth-gilead, or shall I refrain?" And they said,
"Go up, for the LORD will give it into the hand of the king."
But Jehoshaphat said, "Is there not here another prophet of
the LORD of whom we may inquire?" And the king of Israel
said to Jehoshaphat, "There is yet one man by whom we may
inquire of the LORD, Micaiah the son of Imlah, but I hate
him, for he never prophesies good concerning me, but evil."

---

11 • Josephus, Flavius, and Whiston, William (1737). Anitquities of the Jews - Book VIII Ch 14 par 5. In *The Genuine Works of Flavius Josephus the Jewish Historian*.

Micaiah was probably still in prison when Ahab had him summoned to court. On the way to court, the messenger advised Micaiah to tell the king the same thing the "false" prophets were telling him, that is, to go to battle for victory is assured.

I Kings 22:13 (ESV)
And the messenger who went to summon Micaiah said to him, "Behold, the words of the prophets with one accord are favorable to the king. Let your word be like the word of one of them, and speak favorably."

Micaiah responded to his escort that he would only speak what God told him.

I Kings 22:14 (ESV)
But Micaiah said, "As the LORD lives, what the LORD says to me, that I will speak."

Some people have found the comments that Micaiah stated in front of the king as confusing. Look at his words.

I Kings 22:15-17 (ESV)
And when he had come to the king, the king said to him, "Micaiah, shall we go to Ramoth-gilead to battle, or shall we refrain?" And he answered him, "Go up and triumph; the LORD will give it into the hand of the king." But the king said to him, "How many times shall I make you swear that you speak to me nothing but the truth in the name of the LORD?" And he said, "I saw all Israel scattered on the mountains, as sheep that have no shepherd. And the LORD said, 'These have no master; let each return to his home in peace.'

It appears at first glance that Micaiah yielded to peer pressure. His statement was the same as the false prophets. But this is not the case. Judging from Ahab's response, and later the response of the false prophet Zedekiah the son of Chenaanah, Micaiah was making fun of and mocking the false prophets. He was using sarcasm and mockery in his statement to go to victory. Eventually he became serious and made plain his message that the battle would be a victory.

However, look at what he has the guts to tell Ahab.

I Kings 22:17-23 (ESV)

*And he said, "I saw all Israel scattered on the mountains, as sheep that have no shepherd. And the L*ORD *said, 'These have no master; let each return to his home in peace.'"*
*And the king of Israel said to Jehoshaphat, "Did I not tell you that he would not prophesy good concerning me, but evil?" And Micaiah said, "Therefore hear the word of the L*ORD*: I saw the L*ORD *sitting on his throne, and all the host of heaven standing beside him on his right hand and on his left; and the L*ORD *said, 'Who will entice Ahab, that he may go up and fall at Ramoth-gilead?' And one said one thing, and another said another. Then a spirit came forward and stood before the L*ORD*, saying, 'I will entice him.' And the L*ORD *said to him, 'By what means?' And he said, 'I will go out, and will be a lying spirit in the mouth of all his prophets.' And he said, 'You are to entice him, and you shall succeed; go out and do so.' Now therefore behold, the L*ORD *has put a lying spirit in the mouth of all these your prophets; the L*ORD *has declared disaster for you."*

I like this part of the story. It shows a real man who was not afraid to stand up for truth! Today we see too many people twist and perverse the truth simply to make things politically correct or to "fit in" with the right crowd. In verse six we read that there were about 400 false prophets declaring a great victory. These prophets were under the influence of demonic forces. In verse eleven their leader even went to the extreme to make some special decorations (iron horns) for the occasion. Even so, this man of God did not wear a mask or even quiver on the truth. Standing up in front of everyone, he openly declared the truth. He did not sugar coat it to make it gentle on everyone's ears. He told it as it was. He did not distort the truth. This indicates that Micaiah was not afraid of standing up for the truth when hundreds were saying something different. Forget peer pressure or social niceties. This man would not bow to a distortion of the truth. He was wearing no mask!

As is true is most cases when a person will not back down from the truth, Micaiah was insulted and punished.

I Kings 22:24 (ESV)
Then Zedekiah the son of Chenaanah came near and struck Micaiah on the cheek and said, "How did the Spirit of the Lord go from me to speak to you?"

How common it is for those who follow God to be persecuted. Zedekiah did not believe Micaiah because everyone in the kingdom knew that Ahab was going to die in Jezreel and not at this battle in Ramoth-Gilead. (Jezreel is about 45 miles due west of Ramoth-Gilead.) This prophecy came from Elijah, whom even Zedekiah knew was a powerful and truth-speaking prophet.

I Kings 21:17-19 (ESV)
Then the word of the Lord came to Elijah the Tishbite, saying, "Arise, go down to meet Ahab king of Israel, who is in Samaria; behold, he is in the vineyard of Naboth, where he has gone to take possession. And you shall say to him, 'Thus says the Lord, "Have you killed and also taken possession?"' And you shall say to him, 'Thus says the Lord: "In the place where dogs licked up the blood of Naboth shall dogs lick your own blood."'"

From this prophecy we know that King Ahab was going to die at Jezreel, not at Ramoth-Gilead. It would appear that Micaiah might have been wrong in saying that King Ahab would die in this battle. But we shall see that both prophets of God, Elijah and Micaiah, were correct.

So how does our man Micaiah respond to this criticism?

I Kings 22:25 (ESV)
And Micaiah said, "Behold, you shall see on that day when you go into an inner chamber to hide yourself."

Many people find this response confusing. What was Micaiah talking about? Zedekiah had distorted the truth. He said that Ahab would live and be victorious at Ramoth-Gilead. Even so,

Map derived from Erp / Wikimedia, CC BY-SA 4.0 & Nelson's Complete
Book of Bible Maps & Charts. (1996). Thomas Nelson.

Zedekiah knew as everyone else that Ahab would die at Jezreel as Elijah had said years ago. Because of this, Zedekiah could reason as most that Ahab would be victorious at Ramoth-Gilead. But Micaiah was saying that Ahab would die as a result of this battle. He did not say his death would be at Ramoth-Gilead, but that Ahab would die because of that battle. This would prove to everyone that Zedekiah was lying about all of this. It would disgrace him, and he would go into hiding. Again, the historian Josephus tells us about this:

> But Zedekiah, one of those false prophets, came near, and exhorted him not to hearken to Micaiah, for he did not at all speak truth; as a demonstration of which, he instanced in what Elijah had said, who was a better prophet in foretelling futurities than Micaiah; for he foretold that the dogs should lick his blood in the city of Jezreel, in the field of Naboth, as they licked the blood of Naboth, who by his means was there stoned to death by the multitude; that therefore it was plain that this Micaiah was a liar, as contradicting a greater prophet than himself, and saying that he should be slain at three days' journey distance... but Micaiah replied, that Zedekiah, in a few days, should go from one secret chamber to another, to hide himself, that he might escape the punishment of his lying.[12]

Micaiah, under arrest again, was escorted to prison.

I Kings 22:26-28
And the king of Israel said, "Seize Micaiah, and take him back to Amon the governor of the city and to Joash the king's son, and say, 'Thus says the king, "Put this fellow in prison and feed him meager rations of bread and water, until I come in peace."'" "And Micaiah said, "If you return in peace, the LORD has not spoken by me." And he said, "Hear, all you peoples!"

This is the last we read of Micaiah, but it is not the last about wearing a disguise. Ahab was in doubt now about what to do.

12 • Josephus, Flavius, and Whiston, William (1737). *Anitquities of the Jews* - Book VIII Ch 15 par 4. In *The Genuine Works of Flavius Josephus the Jewish Historian.*

He had been told that he would be victorious in battle, but that he would die as a result of the battle. He was not totally trusting Micaiah. After all, he is one prophet opposed to 400. Even so, he made a strange request of King Jehoshaphat.

I Kings 22:29-30 (ESV)
So the king of Israel and Jehoshaphat the king of Judah went up to Ramoth-gilead. And the king of Israel said to Jehoshaphat, "I will disguise myself and go into battle, but you wear your robes." And the king of Israel disguised himself and went into battle.

Ahab was now going to wear a disguise. He dressed like an ordinary soldier. Josephus records that Ahab talked Jehoshaphat into wearing his own kingly robes and go into the battle dressed as Ahab.

Now Ahab and Jehoshaphat had agreed that Ahab should lay aside his royal robes, but that the king of Jerusalem should put on his [Ahab's] proper habit, and stand before the army, in order to disprove, by this artifice, what Micaiah had foretold.[13]

Before the battle began, Ben-Hadad had ordered his men to single Ahab out and kill him. But with King Jehoshaphat wearing Ahab's robes, they pursued the wrong man. Before reaching Jehoshaphat, they saw their mistake and turned away. But one soldier, (Josephus tells us his name was Naaman, who appears in another Bible story), shot an arrow at random into the air and it struck Ahab, mortally wounding him. Ahab left the battle and headed for home in Jezreel, where he died, fulfilling the prophecy of Elijah and Micaiah.

Ahab wore the disguise of a common soldier, but God would not allow his disguise to save him. Disguises are common in the church as well. Some people wear them too well and too often.

---

13 • Josephus, Flavius, and Whiston, William (1737). Anitquities of the Jews - Book VIII Ch 15 par 5. In *The Genuine Works of Flavius Josephus the Jewish Historian.*

Even so, God knows who they really are. It is sad that some people wear a disguise when it comes to their walk with God. Here is a story that illustrates this distressing fact.

Chuck Swindoll tells a story about "Lorne Sanny, of the Navigators, years ago, ministering on the campus of the Air Force Academy where officers in the making are being trained. The campus was filled with competition and peer pressure. One young man who got a Bible class going was very much involved in its success, and it seemed as though month after month the whole thing revolved around him. He continued to keep it going by pushing and motivating others to be involved. Finally, the group grew, and he was the acknowledged leader.

On one occasion early one morning as Lorne was talking with the group about the importance of devotion and time with God, he said, "Young man (called the leader's name), tell us about your walk. Tell us what it is that keeps your heart warm." The young leader blinked a few times through tears and looked around. Against the pressure of the moment he said, "Sir, I don't have any time with God." He said, "As a matter of fact, I'm a fake." And he admitted in front of the whole group that he was simply driven by this need to be known and viewed as the leader, when in reality there was no authenticity behind it."[14]

You may be shocked by this story, but you shouldn't be. People have been wearing disguises and faking their Christianity since the first century. What about you? Are you wearing a disguise to fit in?

Fan the Flame

Christians come in all shapes and sizes. Some go about their business quietly, rarely speaking about spiritual matters. Others are vocal in their church but not out in public. And there are also those who are known for their spiritual beliefs at church

14 • Swindoll, C. R. (1998). Authenticity. In *Swindoll's Ultimate book of illustrations & quotes: Over 1,500 outstanding ways to effectively drive home your message* (pp. 40). T. Nelson.

and in public. Yet do we really know what goes on in the inside? Many times, Christians are called hypocrites because their actions don't align with their speech. Of course, all Christians err one way or another and non-believers need to be reminded that Christians are human, too, and make mistakes. Although their actions should always mesh with God's Word, their actions don't always reflect the truth of God.

Peer pressure can be a dangerous thing when it comes to our Christian beliefs and how we live our lives. It doesn't matter whether peer pressure comes from other Christians or non-believers. Look what happened to a couple named Ananias and Sapphira. Read Acts 4:32 – 5:10. The passage in Acts 4 shows how the early church members took care of each other. Make a note of what was happening among them.

The passage in Acts 5 is about a couple of church members. What did they do that differed from the people in Acts 4?

Here is a couple that wanted to have the same prestige as Barnabas and others. They wanted their fellow believers to think highly of them. It was so important that they concocted a lie and told Peter what they were giving was the price of the land they sold. They could have told Peter it was just part of the sale price and Peter would have accepted it. That lie cost them their lives as an example to the early church.

How do you appear to others? Take a close look at how you portray yourself; include every group you interact with, as we act differently in different situations. Does your outward manifestation truly reflect your heart? If not, what group are you "living a lie" among and what are you covering up? Do you know why?

It's important to be honest with ourselves. I Samuel 16:7b says:

> *"For the LORD sees not as man sees: man looks on the outward appearance, but the LORD looks on the heart."*

Nadab & Abihu
Present Cultures Overrule Some of God's Standards

Leviticus 10:1-7

In his book *What Jesus Said About Successful Living*, Haddon Robinson wrote an interesting story I would like to share with you. Years ago, Joe Bayly, the late Eternity magazine columnist, visited some German Christians who had been devoted German soldiers in the German army during World War II. Two of them had been put up for promotion to become second lieutenants in the Nazi army. The commandant told them he would approve the promotion on one condition: that they join the Officer's Club. Being a member of the club would require them to attend some weekend dances. These young men believed that dancing was wrong because it could lead to immorality. Because of their convictions, they turned down the promotion.

Later in their military careers these men were assigned to death camps where thousands of Jews were stuffed into ovens and killed. Even though they did not directly participate in the slaughter, they knew what was going on. Yet, they never voiced any protest.

When Joe Bayly talked to them many years after the war, they looked back on their experiences with no regret, convinced that they had made good decisions. For them, not conforming to social pressure and refusing to dance was an act of righteousness. Conforming to patriotic, mass murder and remaining silent while thousands of Jews burned in ovens left them with no feelings of unrighteousness.

When we set our own standard of external righteousness, we are capable of any evil. When we are filled with His righteousness, no good is too great.

Sometimes, Christians struggle with truth. Yes, they know what God's Word contains and what it is, yet they will set their own standards. They may justify this by saying that God's Word was written for an ancient Jewish culture, and it does not apply to America or the world today. Sure, the way of salvation is still true, but the other messages and commands do not necessarily pertain to our culture today. Thus, they set their own standards to live by, neglecting God's Word.

I believe that God and His Word are the same yesterday, today, and tomorrow! I believe that we are not to alter His Word to try to fit it into our own standards. I truly believe that if we all live by His standards, how blessed our nation would be. I also believe that many of our young people would not be compromising personal integrity and thus would have fewer pressures. Two non-popular biblical characters who illustrate God's unchanging character are Nadab and Abihu, two older sons of Aaron the High Priest during the exodus.

Exodus 6:23 (ESV)
Aaron took as his wife Elisheba, the daughter of Amminadab and the sister of Nahshon, and she bore him Nadab, Abihu, Eleazar, and Ithamar.

Thus, they were priests. Priests were given the privilege to serve God.

Exodus 28:1 (ESV)
"Then bring near to you Aaron your brother, and his sons with him, from among the people of Israel,

to serve me as priests—Aaron and Aaron's sons,
Nadab and Abihu, Eleazar and Ithamar.

These two special men were allowed to go up on Mt. Sinai with Moses and Aaron.

Exodus 24:9 (ESV)
Then Moses and Aaron, Nadab, and Abihu, and seventy
of the elders of Israel went up [to Mt. Sinai].

These men were allowed the great privilege of seeing the feet of God.

Exodus 24:10 (ESV)
And they saw the God of Israel. There was
under his feet as it were a pavement of sapphire
stone, like the very heaven for clearness.

These two men were given the privilege to wear special priestly garments, different from other priests.

Exodus 28:4 (ESV)
These are the garments that they shall make: a breastpiece,
an ephod, a robe, a coat of checker work, a turban,
and a sash. They shall make holy garments for Aaron
your brother and his sons to serve me as priests.

In chapter 9 of Leviticus, we find Aaron, Nadab, and Abihu all working and performing their priestly duties as commanded by God. A series of sacrifices had been performed and the people were astonished by God's answer for those sacrifices.

Leviticus 9:23-24 (ESV)
And Moses and Aaron went into the tent of meeting, and
when they came out they blessed the people, and the
glory of the LORD appeared to all the people. And fire
came out from before the LORD and consumed the burnt
offering and the pieces of fat on the altar, and when all
the people saw it, they shouted and fell on their faces.

Nadab and Abihu were wearing their special garments and assisting their dad as the Lord commanded. Everything was proceeding according to God's directives and the people were being blessed. But suddenly, something went terribly wrong.

Leviticus 10:1-2 (ESV)
Now Nadab and Abihu, the sons of Aaron, each took his censer and put fire in it and laid incense on it and offered unauthorized fire before the LORD, which he had not commanded them. And fire came out from before the LORD and consumed them, and they died before the LORD.

Both Nadab and Abihu experienced spontaneous human combustion. Why? Everything was going so well, the people were being blessed, and God was receiving praise. What happened? As they were working, Nadab and Abihu used **unauthorized** fire for their censers. What does that mean? Looking back at the ancient Hebrew text the word for **unauthorized** is: זוּר zuwr, pronounced "zoor" meaning, strange or profane. It is the same word used for "commit adultery."

What did Nadab & Abihu do wrong? We are not specifically told what they did that was against God's instructions. Some scholars believe that they were drunk when performing their duties since a prohibition against drinking appears soon afterwards in the chapter. Other scholars believe that the coals they used to burn the incense were obtained from a different source than where God commanded since the word **strange** is used to describe it. In any case, they disobeyed God and substituted what they thought was "just as good." Actually, they were guilty of three offenses. First, they used a profane and unholy fire in their censers. Second, they did not do what God had commanded. Third, they set their own standards of what was right and acceptable. Notice, the task did not change. The fire they used would still burn the incense. The result would be the same, ashes. But by setting their own truths and criterion, their own interpretation of worshipping God, they sinned.

How did God react to these men changing His Word and commands? First, God kept His standards. He is perfect and does not make mistakes. He is bound by His own Word to do what He says. He is not like mankind that changes, even if world cultures and society changes. God cannot change (Malachi 3:6). He does not conform to man's interpretation. This is contrary to what many people think today that God must keep up with man's changing culture.

Second, God proved that His Word is not to be trifled with. Man is not to change God's commands to fit his own ideas or personal viewpoints, a sin that is very popular today. I often hear people tell me that God's perspective on certain sins is not relevant today in our modern society.

Leviticus 10:3 (ESV)
"This is what the LORD has said, 'Among those who are near me I will be sanctified, and before all the people I will be glorified'"

Third, God explained to Moses that anyone disregarding His commands offends Him and disrespects Him. That is of course a sin. God is saying that He is to be honored and respected by everyone. After all, He is the Creator and He is Almighty God, fully deserving this. Who is man to decide how Almighty God thinks?

Fourth, God showed the consequences of man compromising His Word. Man is in no position to correct Almighty God when we disagree with what He says. God will be glorified before all of creation and to insult God or show Him contempt meets with disaster and death. God used this example of Nadab and Abihu to show the people that He will not allow personal interpretation of His Law.

Can you imagine what must have gone through Aaron's mind when God pronounced judgment on his sons Nadab and Abihu? Think for a moment about what Eleazer and Ithamar witnessed and thought when they saw their brothers burst into flames. They just saw their brothers burnt to a crisp right before their eyes. I know some people today react with severe anger towards God when loved ones are punished by God or are taken away due to their sins. We all sin and are unrighteous before God. What amazes me is how patient and merciful God is with us when we do sin.

How did the relatives and people react when God pronounced judgment on Nadab and Abihu? First, they were told not to mourn them. It would be a rebellious thing to do in light of God's judgment on this sin. The nation of Israel would have viewed mourning or honoring their deaths as a lack of respect towards God.

Leviticus 10:6 (ESV)
And Moses said to Aaron and to Eleazar and Ithamar his sons, "Do not let the hair of your heads hang loose, and do not tear your clothes, lest you die, and wrath come upon all the congregation; but let your brothers, the whole house of Israel, bewail the burning that the Lord has kindled.

Second, they were told to continue in their work at that time. God's commands are to be honored. They are the most important items on our agendas. To defy Almighty God and honor these two dead men would be appalling and lead to more disobedience.

Leviticus 10:7 (ESV)
And do not go outside the entrance of the tent of meeting, lest you die, for the anointing oil of the Lord is upon you." And they did according to the word of Moses.

They were involved in an act of worshipping God and were not to halt that because of the judgment poured out on Nadab and Abihu.

Third, they were not allowed to even carry the charred bodies away. Again, this could be seen as a means of honoring them and they are the example of how serious a matter it is to obey God in every detail.

Leviticus 10:4-5 (ESV)
And Moses called Mishael and Elzaphan, the sons of Uzziel the uncle of Aaron, and said to them, "Come near; carry your brothers away from the front of the sanctuary and out of the camp." So they came near and carried them in their coats out of the camp, as Moses had said.

Nadab and Abihu's cousins had the job of carrying the charred remains outside of camp to be disposed of in the rubbish heap. Again, these two individuals were not to be honored.

Eleazar and Ithamar would now serve in the roles of these two disobedient priests. The two dead priests were replaced by their brothers.

Numbers 3:4 (ESV)
But Nadab and Abihu died before the Lord when they offered unauthorized fire before the Lord in the wilderness of Sinai, and they had no children. So Eleazar and Ithamar served as priests in the lifetime of Aaron their father.

What can we learn from these two minor characters? What lessons do they teach us in our walk with Almighty God? I believe there are several lessons we can learn from this story God placed in His Word.

First, God's Word is not to be tampered with. Today, many people, and even some preachers from the pulpits, teach that God's Word is not perfect, it is culturally variable. It is fluctuating, inconsistent, and open to various interpretations. They even preach that modern societies and cultural changes influence it. This tactic of the enemy is old. Even Paul faced such challenges, for he wrote to the Corinthian church:

II Corinthians 4:2 (GW)
We don't distort God's word.

A second lesson we can learn from this is that God's Word is the standard of judgment. God does not treat nicely and softly those who distort, change, or use personal ideas over God's explicit commands. He will judge those people who are called to serve Him under a more severe standard. People who are leaders in the church will be held more responsible and judged more harshly than laymen.

James 3:1 (ESV)
Not many of you should become teachers, my brothers, for you know that we who teach will be judged with greater strictness.

Third, do not add to or take away from God's Word. In other words, don't distort God's Word. Society and cultures cannot change God or His Word. So why do some people think that their opinions matter more than God's? God is immutable, holy, and perfect. You don't change perfection.

Deuteronomy 4:2 (ESV)
You shall not add to the word that I command you, nor take from it, that you may keep the commandments of the LORD your God that I command you.

Deuteronomy 12:32 (ESV)
"Everything that I command you, you shall be careful to do. You shall not add to it or take from it.

Revelation 22:18-19 (ESV)
I warn everyone who hears the words of the prophecy of this book: if anyone adds to them, God will add to him the plagues described in this book, and if anyone takes away from the words of the book of this prophecy, God will take away his share in the tree of life and in the holy city, which are described in this book.

Lastly, we must respect the Word of God. True, there are some commands in the Old Covenant that do not apply to us today as Christians because they were fulfilled by Jesus. But the New Covenant repeats many of the Laws, such as the Ten Commandments, and others, and we are not to challenge or change these.

Luke 11:28 (ESV)
But he said, "Blessed rather are those who hear the word of God and keep it!"

Hebrews 4:12 (ESV)
For the word of God is living and active, sharper than any two-edged sword, piercing to the division of soul and of spirit, of joints and of marrow, and discerning the thoughts and intentions of the heart.

The Scriptures are the Word of God. In them He has given us the chart to steer our souls through the reefs of humanism and degradation. Sailing your life by its course will bring you successfully into the safe harbor of God's open arms. But people will always challenge authorities for their own interpretations.

Those who were born before 1970 may well remember the May 18th, 1980, eruption of Mt. St. Helens in Washington. For months the U.S. Geological Survey had been warning people to stay away from the mountain as it was showing signs of a possible violent eruption. Many heeded the warnings, instructions, and rules and evacuated the area. Fifty-seven people didn't. The most famous was a man named Harry Randall Truman.

Harry Randall Truman was 83 years old and a widow. He owned a lodge on beautiful Spirit Lake near Mt. St. Helens. For weeks he was urged and ordered to evacuate, but he had felt rumbles from that mountain before and was determined to stay. He became a celebrity for his insistence to stay with his 16 cats. He was interviewed on T.V. and even *National Geographic* ran an article on him. The colorful man with his vulgar expletives was so popular, and he had quite a following of people supporting him. But at 8:23 a.m. on that fateful day, he paid the full penalty for his disobedience for not following directives by officials when his home was hit by an avalanche of hot ash, mud, and more. His lodge was obliterated, and his remains were never found.

Challenging the authority of government laws is one thing but inserting your own interpretations and challenging God's direct commands is another. The Bible is the Creator's guideline to an abundant life, but also holds the key to eternal life. We would do well to follow what God has told us and listen less to man's interpretation.

Fan the Flame

Do you believe that parts of Scripture are no longer valid to today's living? List these areas and give an explanation of why you believe it.

Read Isaiah 55:8-9 and see what God has to say about our ability to set the rules.

Why is it important for believers to follow Scripture? Write down II Timothy 3:16-17, and words that Jesus Himself spoke Matthew 5:48.

What does the future hold for mankind? Revelation 20:11-12 explains that we all, good and bad, will have to give an accounting of our lives. Are you ready to make your argument to the perfect Judge?

How did people's belief systems change? Everyone agrees that we now accept certain behavior that a few decades ago people would find appalling. I believe Christians are largely responsible for it. Have you noticed something that is contrary to God's Word but you did or said nothing about it? It did, or will become, the norm for lack of opposition. Speaking the name of God in a derogatory manner, the way we dress, the gathering of people together are just the tip of the iceberg of things that slid by unchallenged. Even the hot topics today of homosexuality and abortion are being challenged. Should we sit by and do nothing and let our country slide even further away from God? Are you willing to stand up for your God?

II Chronicles 7:14 (KJV)
If my people, which are called by my name, shall humble themselves, and pray, and seek my face, and turn from their wicked ways; then will I hear from heaven, and will forgive their sin, and will heal their land.

Jehoiada
When No One Holds You Accountable

II Chronicles 22 - 24

Some years ago, I worked at a school plagued by low ACT and SAT scores. The principal was bothered by the underachieving students. When I came to the school to interview for a biology teaching position, the principal told me about the low tests scores. He explained that there were too many teachers on tenure who were not teaching to their potential. He seemed to say that there was not much he could do about it since they were tenured. I asked to see the scores for the past few years, which he proceeded to show me. Math was low, but science was in the basement. He looked me straight in the eye and said, "If I hire you to lead this department, what can you do about these scores?" I leaned back and said that if he would do two things, I thought I could raise the scores in science up 10% in three years. I then proceeded to say, "If you agree to my demands on this and the scores do not improve by at least 10% in three years, I will resign." He asked me what my two demands were, and I said that first I needed the science budget to double. (The current budget was under $2,000.) The second thing was for him to observe me. I asked him to come into my class as often as possible, even if he could only spare a few minutes. He agreed to my terms, and

I was hired. Though he did not come into my classes as much as I wanted, he often stood outside the door so I could see him but the students could not. If he could not come in and observe me, he sent the assistant principal.

Accountability was what I desired. I knew I would do a better job if I was being observed.

While I taught there, I discovered that a colleague of mine seldom did any teaching. He often would walk around his room and check to see if the students had done their homework, then he would have them grade it in class. Then he would instruct the students to read a section in the textbook silently and complete either the odd or even problems. As the students sat doing work, he would sit back in his big chair and read a novel.

That colleague and I would often talk about how the administrators were constantly observing me but not him. He once asked me if I was in trouble or if being observed that frequently annoyed me. I told him that I asked for this treatment as it would hold me accountable. He thought I was nuts. He said that he could never be the teacher he was if he was observed like that.

Accountability is something that really helps us improve and develop, not only in our occupation, but also in our spiritual lives. Having another Christian hold us accountable and walk alongside us can help us grow and mature into stronger and more effective Christians.

For more than two decades, I worked at a Christian camp in the Northwoods of Wisconsin. I taught weekly Bible studies and was the spiritual leader for the volunteer summer staff there. I often taught them material to help them face the world outside of camp. I tried to prepare them for taking their Christian faith into a fallen world while remaining close to Christ after they left the comfortable Christian environment the camp offered. I often kept in contact with many to help guide them after they left. While working there, I noticed that many grew strong in their faith through the close contact with great staff leaders. They thrived spiritually during camp. However, I was alarmed to find that many experienced a drought in their faith after leaving the confines of the Christian environment.

Again, God's Word has a lesson here for us. It concerns the popular Bible story of a boy-king who was saved from death by his aunt.

II Chronicles 22:10-12 (ESV)
Now when Athaliah the mother of Ahaziah saw that her son was dead, she arose and destroyed all the royal family of the house of Judah. But Jehoshabeath, the daughter of the king, took Joash the son of Ahaziah and stole him away from among the king's sons who were about to be put to death, and she put him and his nurse in a bedroom. Thus Jehoshabeath, the daughter of King Jehoram and wife of Jehoiada the priest, because she was a sister of Ahaziah, hid him from Athaliah, so that she did not put him to death. And he remained with them six years, hidden in the house of God, while Athaliah reigned over the land.

Young Joash's aunt and uncle rescued him from death by hiding him in the temple. We can assume he was about one year old because his nurse was hidden with him.

Something that could be overlooked here is that Athaliah, an idolator who did not worship God, tried to do more than just become the ruler of Judah. She was, in fact, trying to destroy God's plan of the Messiah. She was at war with God. Knowing the messianic prophecies, she attempted to destroy the line of David forever, thus ending Yahweh worship for all time. But man cannot war with God and expect to win.

As the popular Sunday school story goes, Jehoiada the priest presented Joash as king in the Temple when he was only seven years old. The wicked Athaliah was killed in the royal stables among the manure. It was a fitting end to such a person who made the country smell in God's nostrils. Then Jehoiada does something special with the new king and people.

II Chronicles 23:16-19 (ESV)

And Jehoiada made a covenant between himself and all the people and the king that they should be the LORD's people. Then all the people went to the house of Baal and tore it down; his altars and his images they broke in pieces, and they killed Mattan the priest of Baal before the altars. And Jehoiada posted watchmen for the house of the LORD under the direction of the Levitical priests and the Levites whom David had organized to be in charge of the house of the LORD, to offer burnt offerings to the LORD, as it is written in the Law of Moses, with rejoicing and with singing, according to the order of David. He stationed the gatekeepers at the gates of the house of the LORD so that no one should enter who was in any way unclean.

After Athaliah was disposed of, Jehoiada immediately began making spiritual reforms. He reestablished a covenant to be the Lord's people. They didn't just say this with their words, but their actions. They destroyed the temple of Baal and executed the priest. Joash followed God's command about temple worship and reinstated the Levites and priests to their duties as commanded by Moses and David. He repaired and cleaned the Temple of God.

So goes the popular Bible story. But the story does not end here. It continued with highlights but has a strange twist at the end.

As long as Jehoiada was alive, King Joash followed God's command. Positive influence is a powerful thing as demonstrated by the impact King Joash's uncle made in his life. A teacher should be a positive influence on students. That is why teaching is a very noble calling. It is not for everyone. As you will recall, James 3:1 contains a warning for teachers.

James 3:1 (ESV)

Not many of you should become teachers, my brothers, for you know that we who teach will be judged with greater strictness.

Someone said, "Those who can, teach. Those who can't, go into another less significant occupation." Maybe that is why national news often carries stories about teachers stumbling and plunging into appalling situations. Only parents influence more people than teachers.

II Chronicles 24:1-4 (ESV)

Joash was seven years old when he began to reign, and he reigned forty years in Jerusalem. His mother's name was Zibiah of Beersheba. And Joash did what was right in the eyes of the LORD all the days of Jehoiada the priest. Jehoiada got for him two wives, and he had sons and daughters. After this Joash decided to restore the house of the Lord.

I want to focus on verse two of this passage and this time, let's examine it from a different translation.

II Chronicles 24:2 (GW)

Joash did what the LORD considered right, as long as the priest Jehoiada lived.

Did you notice that young Joash had an accountability partner? Let's examine what influences he had on this young king.

First, Jehoiada raised him in the Temple of God. Going to the Temple would be similar to us going to church today. That was where people gathered to corporately worship and praise God. In a way, we might say today that Joash grew up in church. Going to church is not only good for Christians today, but it is commanded by God in Hebrews 10:25.

Second, his uncle Jehoiada taught him God's Word frequently. Having daily Bible studies with God was a way of life for him, and it should be for us, too. It amazes me how many people long to hear God speak to them and never open up the 66 love letters He gave telling us how to live.

Third, Jehoiada taught him to pray often. The Temple was the House of Prayer. Prayer is a key for growing spiritually.

Fourth, Jehoiada taught him to sacrifice to God. Joash grew up witnessing daily sacrifices being offered to God; an act of worship. Thus, he grew up worshipping God.

Fifth, Jehoiada guided Joash in his job as king. Joash had a godly man watching over him daily, answering his questions and yielding advice.

Sixth, Jehoiada showed Joash how to set priorities in life. He was raised with the Word of God as his conscience. King Joash demonstrated this when he was frustrated by the slow progress of repairs to God's Temple.

II Chronicles 24:6 (ESV)
So the king summoned Jehoiada the chief and said to him, "Why have you not required the Levites to bring in from Judah and Jerusalem the tax levied by Moses, the servant of the LORD, and the congregation of Israel for the tent of testimony?"

Seventh, from this same verse we read that Joash learned how to tithe and was faithful in this. Joash learned that giving to the Lord is a form of worship.

Eighth, Jehoiada guided young Joash in his dating life and helped him find two good wives. I am not saying that men should have two wives; some men struggle being a good husband to one.

Ninth, Jehoiada taught Joash how to be a good father to his children. We read in II Chronicles 25:2, that his son Amaziah was considered a good king. Clearly Joash raised him to be a good leader. Jehoiada had a major influence on this young man.

We should all have some person who can observe us frequently and hold us accountable. As with all people, Jehoiada was human, and this godly man died. When he died, King Joash had him buried in the royal cemetery, which was a great honor.

II Chronicles 24:15-16 (ESV)
But Jehoiada grew old and full of days, and died. He

*was 130 years old at his death. And they buried him
in the city of David among the kings, because he had
done good in Israel, and toward God and his house.*

Let's review the obvious here because it is so important. As long as King Joash had his uncle Jehoiada beside him to guide him, his spiritual growth and devotion to God was untarnished.

This is why many young people who work in a Christian environment have a spiritual advantage and why I encourage young people to get involved with a good, biblical Christian environment like a camp or study group.

What are these spiritual advantages? Let's examine them briefly.

Students are encouraged and challenged in Bible reading, study, and prayer. Distracting devices are removed and pressures from social issues are more easily handled with mentors alongside. Students feel a sense of belonging as well as have the opportunity to be spiritually fed from Bible teachers.

The sad part of this story is what happens after Jehoiada dies.

II Chronicles 24:17-19 (ESV)
*Now after the death of Jehoiada the princes of Judah
came and paid homage to the king. Then the king listened
to them. And they abandoned the house of the LORD,
the God of their fathers, and served the Asherim and
the idols. And wrath came upon Judah and Jerusalem
for this guilt of theirs. Yet he sent prophets among
them to bring them back to the LORD. These testified
against them, but they would not pay attention.*

The words "princes of Judah" do not mean the sons of Joash. The Hebrew word "princes" used here is רַשׁ **sar**, meaning a head person, an official, a captain, a chief, a general, or a governor. So, it was people that were the social elite or leaders. Another translation puts it this way:

II Chronicles 24:17 (GW)
After he died, the officials of Judah bowed in front
of the king with their faces touching the ground.
Then the king listened to their advice.

King Joash turns to them for advice and counsel. They quickly turn him away from worshipping Yahweh to instead worship *Asherim.*

Who was *Asherim*? She was the idol called *Asherah*, the Phoenician goddess of love and seduction. She was strongly worshipped by Queen Jezebel, who was from Phoenicia. Asherah was the consort of Baal. Worshipping her involved sexual orgies performed in public. Shockingly, idol worship was reinstituted in Judah by the very man who demolished it and prohibited it just years before.

We learn what can happen when the person holding you accountable is absent. The story gets even worse. Many prophets were sent to call Joash back to the Lord, but they all failed. Then God sent Joash's cousin, the son of Joash's tutor, to call him back to the Lord.

II Chronicles 24:20-22 (ESV)
Then the Spirit of God clothed Zechariah the son of Jehoiada
the priest, and he stood above the people, and said to them,
"Thus says God, 'Why do you break the commandments of
the LORD, so that you cannot prosper? Because you have
forsaken the LORD, he has forsaken you.'" But they conspired
against him, and by command of the king they stoned him
with stones in the court of the house of the LORD. Thus Joash
the king did not remember the kindness that Jehoiada,
Zechariah's father, had shown him, but killed his son. And
when he was dying, he said, "May the Lord see and avenge!"

How did King Joash reward his mentor and teacher Jehoiada? The king himself signed the contract to have his son murdered! Because of this, God allowed King Joash to come under attack from the Syrian army that conquered Judah.

II Chronicles 24:24 (ESV)
Though the army of the Syrians had come with few men, the LORD delivered into their hand a very great army, because Judah had forsaken the LORD, the God of their fathers. Thus they executed judgment on Joash.

During this battle, King Joash was wounded. As he was recovering, he was murdered on his bed for issuing the decree to have his cousin Zechariah, the son of his mentor Jehoiada, executed.

II Chronicles 24:25 (ESV)
When they had departed from him, leaving him severely wounded, his servants conspired against him because of the blood of the son of Jehoiada the priest, and killed him on his bed. So he died, and they buried him in the city of David, but they did not bury him in the tombs of the kings.

Did you catch that King Joash was not even buried in the royal tombs of the other kings? He had changed so much that he was not even honored in death. It is interesting that although his mentor was buried there, the king himself was not.

Here concludes a great example of the importance of accountability. As long as Joash's mentor was present, he followed the Lord. When separated from Jehoiada, he fell away into sin and darkness.

In his book, *There's a Lot More to Health Than Not Being Sick*, Bruce Larson writes: Behavioral sciences in recent years have expounded the simple truth that "behavior that is observed changes." People who are accountable by their own choice to a group of friends, to a therapy group, to a psychiatrist or a pastoral counselor, to a study group, or prayer group, are people who are serious about changing their behavior, and they are finding that change is possible.

Studies done in factories have proven that both quality and quantity of work increases when the employees know they are being observed. If only God knows what I am doing, since I know He won't tell, I tend to make all kinds of excuses for myself. But if I must report to another or a group of others, I begin to monitor my behavior. If someone is keeping an eye on me, my behavior improves.

Fan the Flame

This is a happy yet tragic story of someone who started out gung-ho for God but later turned his back on Him. Do you know of anyone who has done that? Is this the story of your own life? I hope not. If it is, it is never too late to ask forgiveness and return to God. Many young people who have left for college find themselves in the same predicament as Joash. They were faithful attendees of church growing up but once they left the church's and their parents' leadership they find their own faith lacking and easily slip away from God.

Look at these cousins, Joash and Zechariah. Both were under the influence of Jehoiada. Both experienced his teaching and service to God. Yet, the two cousins couldn't have been more different after the death of Jehoiada. Joash turned his back on God and committed murder. Zechariah remained faithful to God and was killed for it.

Influences of a good mentor:
Jot down where you are strong or weak.

1. Raised in a godly church (Hebrews 10:25)

2. Learn Scripture (Acts 22:3)

3. Pray often (Romans 12:12)

4. Sacrifice (Romans 12:1)

5. Have a godly mentor (story of Jehoiada and Joash)

6. Set spiritual priorities (Ephesians 2:10)

7. Tithe (Malachi 3:8-10)

8. Careful in who you date and marry (II Corinthians 6:14)

9. Learn to be a good parent (Deuteronomy 6:6-8)

Aaron

Giving in to Social and Peer Pressures

Exodus 32

In his book, *Living Above the Level of Mediocrity,* Chuck Swindoll cites an interesting story.

> *Once a spider built a beautiful web in an old house. He kept it clean and shiny so that flies would patronize it. The minute he got a "customer" he would clean up after him so that other flies would not get suspicious.*

> *Then one day this fairly intelligent fly came buzzing by the clean spider web. Old man spider called out, "Come in and sit." But the fairly intelligent fly said, "No, sir. I don't see other flies in your house, and I am not going in alone!"*

> *But presently he saw on the floor below a large crowd of flies dancing around on a piece of brown paper. He was delighted! He was not afraid if lots of flies were doing it. So, he came in for a landing.*

> *Just before he landed, a bee zoomed by saying, "Don't land there stupid! That's flypaper!" But the fairly intelligent fly shouted back, "Don't be silly. Those flies are dancing. There's a big crowd there. Everybody's doing it.*

That many flies can't be wrong!" Well, you know what happened. He died on the spot.

Some of us want to be with the crowd so badly that we end up in a mess. What does it profit a fly (or a person) if he escapes the web only to end up in glue?[15]

Do you ever have problems with peer pressure? Most people do at some point in their lives. We see ads on TV, computers, our phones, magazines, newspapers, etc., coaching us about how to handle these things; but even so, this is an area of difficultly for many people, including Christians. Usually, the topics dealing with peer pressure are about drugs, sex, and alcohol abuse. Social pressures often deal with clothing, cars, opinions, and materialism. But one topic that is covered by both peer and social pressures deals with a spiritual walk with God.

"I love being at church because I can show my walk with God here among others who are walking with Him. But at home, work, or at school, I can't show it, or people will think me weird or strange." That is a comment that I have heard many times and one I can understand. When I was a teen, I knew it was common for Christians to be labeled as weird. (Some people today might say time has not changed that.) I realized early in my Christian walk with God that Christians are strange people. I mean, have you ever examined the life of Elijah or John the Baptist closely? They had a close walk with God and were really strange! Scripture describes their appearance alone as quite peculiar. They just did not fit in with their peers or society because these guys were so strong in their faith. But what about people who are not as strong in their faith? One such person who yielded to peer and social pressure was that famous brother of Moses, Aaron.

Who was this Aaron guy? There are a dozen basic facts the Bible records about this famous man. First, he was the older brother of Moses (Exodus 6:20). Second, he was the first high priest of

---

15 • Swindoll, C. R. (1989). In *Living Above the Level of Mediocrity: A commitment to excellence* (pp. 223–224). Word Publishing.

the Hebrew nation (Exodus 28:1). Third, he was Moses' public spokesman (Exodus 4:14-16). Fourth, he was 83 years old when Moses began his ministry (Exodus 7:7). Fifth, he performed miracles before Pharaoh (Exodus 7:10 & 8:6). Sixth, he was present with Moses when God spoke about Passover (Exodus 12:1-20). Seventh, he was a major player in the Exodus from Egypt. Eighth, the people blamed him along with Moses about the harshness of the wilderness (Numbers 14:2). Ninth, he helped maintain order and rendered judgments over the people along with Moses (Numbers 15:32-33). Tenth, he was the supervisor of the Tabernacle and its furnishings (Numbers 4). Eleventh, because he sinned by not upholding God's holiness, he was not allowed to enter the Promised Land. (Numbers 20:12). And twelfth, he died on Mt. Hor after transferring his garments and title to his son Eleazar (Numbers 20:22-29).

Aaron was a major player to the Israelites as the exodus occurred. He was also the high priest of the Hebrew people, though he was quite imperfect. (Jesus Christ is now in the position of priesthood in the order of Melchizedek (Hebrews 5:2-5; 7:11-12).

As important as Aaron was, he did have a major character weakness that manifested itself at Mt. Sinai. He gave into peer and social pressures in an abominable way. Let's set that flawed scene. The Israelites were camped at the base of Mt. Sinai. Moses had ascended the mountain, (with Joshua going part of the way up) and had been gone forty days and nights.

Exodus 24:13-15, 18 (ESV)
So Moses rose with his assistant Joshua, and Moses went up into the mountain of God. And he said to the elders, "Wait here for us until we return to you. And behold, Aaron and Hur are with you. Whoever has a dispute, let him go to them." Then Moses went up on the mountain, and the cloud covered the mountain...Moses entered the cloud and went up on the mountain. And Moses was on the mountain forty days and forty nights.

Moses stated that if a problem arose in the group below, or if the people became restless as Moses was up on the mountain, they could go to Aaron his brother for leadership.

Well, time passed and Aaron was the camp director for forty days. He was the leader in the absence of Moses. After all, he had been beside Moses in leadership and had witnessed mighty miracles: the death of Pharaoh's army, manna appearing mysteriously, quail coming directly into camp, water from a rock in a barren land, and the miraculous defeat of the Amalekites. One would think that the faith of the Israelite nation was really strong. They had experienced what no man had seen before.

This time period in the Israelite camp may be similar to what you experienced when you came to Christ for salvation. Maybe you experienced God's providence and His mighty power over evil. Maybe you heard fantastic sermons or lessons directly from His Word. Maybe you are on fire for God right now, but times of doubt, despair, and perhaps suffering are often right around the corner. I know many men of God who hate Mondays because after seeing God work strongly on Sundays, they feel an absence, and depression easily sets in. Well, the Hebrew nation experienced that too.

Exodus 32:1-6 (NASB)

Now when the people saw that Moses delayed to come down from the mountain, the people assembled about Aaron, and said to him, "Come, make us a god who will go before us; as for this Moses, the man who brought us up from the land of Egypt, we do not know what has become of him." And Aaron said to them, "Tear off the gold rings which are in the ears of your wives, your sons, and your daughters, and bring them to me." Then all the people tore off the gold rings which were in their ears, and brought them to Aaron. And he took this from their hand, and fashioned it with a graving tool, and made it into a molten calf; and they said, "This is your god, O Israel, who brought you up from the land of Egypt." Now when Aaron saw this, he built an altar before it; and Aaron made a proclamation and said, "Tomorrow shall be a feast to the LORD." So the next day they rose early and offered burnt offerings, and brought peace offerings; and the people sat down to eat and to drink, and rose up to play.

Many people incorrectly think that Aaron and the people turned completely away from Yahweh at this time, but that is not exactly what happened. Notice that Aaron says that this is the god whom we have been following. He made God into an image of a calf and proclaimed that this was the same God that they had been following all along through the desert. In verse four, the word for God is מיהלא **Elohim**, the same name for God that is in Genesis 1:1. Also, in verse five the name of God Aaron uses is הָוֹהִי **YHVH** or **Yahweh**, the proper name of God. Even Psalm 106: 19-20 makes it clear that they made an idol for God. They designed

a new way of worshipping God by continuing to call Him LORD but holding a feast with burnt offerings to the calf. The people made the true God into an idol to worship, thereby breaking the commandments God had given them. The Hebrew people were accustomed to seeing idols of every sort in Egypt; archaeologists have found many idols of El and Elohim in the land of Israel.

A 12th century BC bronze idol of El from Samaria, Israel Museum (E4F)

Exodus 20:4-7 (ESV)
"You shall not make for yourself a carved image, or any likeness of anything that is in heaven above, or that is in the earth beneath, or that is in the water under the earth. You shall not bow down to them or serve them, for I the LORD your God am a jealous God, visiting the iniquity of the fathers on the children to the third and the fourth generation of those who hate me, but showing steadfast love to thousands of those who love me and keep my commandments. You shall not take the name of the LORD your God in vain, for the LORD will not hold him guiltless who takes his name in vain."

The people demanded an idol from Aaron that they could see and touch. Aaron was put on the spot, much like what you may face at work or school when questioned about your walk with God. Aaron could have been strong and led the people to what was right and true. But under peer and social pressure – he fell. How exactly did Aaron go wrong and stumble?

Aaron made six basic blunders in his walk with God. First, he gave in to peer pressure and viewed people's opinions higher than God's. Second, he compromised truth in favor for the popular opinion of the people. Third, he did not want to appear different from those around him. There were so many, and he reasoned if that many were saying the same thing, they must be right. He let numbers influence him instead of his heart. Fourth, he did not want to lose the leadership position he had with the people. Fear of demotion will scare many into doing something inappropriate, even if they know it is wrong. Fifth, he chose to follow society instead of following God's Word. That was a huge mistake! Sixth, he made excuses and altered God's Word to fit his own dreams and ideas. That is so prevalent in society today, even in the church! People alter the meaning of God's Word to suit society or their own sinful desires.

Meanwhile, up on the mountain, God knew what was happening back down at the camp and He told Moses to return.

Exodus 32:7-10 (GW)
The Lord said to Moses, "Go back down there. Your people whom you brought out of Egypt have ruined [everything]. They've already turned from the way I commanded them to live. They've made a statue of a calf for themselves. They've bowed down to it and offered sacrifices to it. They've said, 'Israel, here are your gods who brought you out of Egypt.'" The Lord added, "I've seen these people, and they are impossible to deal with. Now leave me alone. I'm so angry with them I am going to destroy them. Then I'll make you into a great nation."

God does not compromise with society. His Word is truth, and He hates sin. He was going to destroy them all and begin a new nation with Moses, but He relented from wiping them out at that time.

Exodus 32:11& 14 (ESV)
*But Moses implored the L*ORD *his God and said, "O L*ORD, *why does your wrath burn hot against your people, whom you have brought out of the land of Egypt with great power and with a mighty hand? ... And the L*ORD *relented from the disaster that he had spoken of bringing on his people.*

The people were spared because Moses intervened for them. This is prophetic and symbolic of what Jesus does for us. Because we sin and disobey God, we are set to die. Yet Christ intervenes for us.

Moses then confronted Aaron.

Exodus 32:21-24 (GW)
Moses asked Aaron, "What did these people do to you that you encouraged them to commit such a serious sin?" "Don't be angry, sir," Aaron answered. "You know that these people are evil. They said to me, 'We don't know what's happened to this Moses who brought us out of Egypt. Make gods for us. They will lead us.' So I told them to take off any gold they were wearing. They gave it to me. I threw it into the fire, and out came this calf!"

Can you believe the excuse Aaron gave Moses? It is an excuse all right. He was trying to get out of this mess by making up a story. A supernatural story. The calf just formed and came out of the fire? Come on, Aaron!

Did you notice what Aaron did when confronted? He made an excuse instead of admitting his failure. He lied. He tried to shift the blame from himself on to the people. He did not accept responsibility for his wrong actions. He was supposed to keep the people encouraged and walking close with God, but instead failed miserably at this. He made excuses for his poor behavior. Does this sound familiar? Have you seen people do the same thing when they mess up? Maybe you have done the same thing Aaron did when confronted by someone about your compromises.

Obviously, Moses was mad, and God was also angry. Look at what is found in Deuteronomy when this event is summarized later.

Deuteronomy 9:20 (GW)
The Lord also became very angry with Aaron and wanted to destroy him. But at that time I prayed for Aaron, too.

God was going to kill Aaron for this sin, but Moses pleaded for his life and God spared him. Does this give you an indication on how God feels when we sinfully yield to peer and social pressure?

The lessons we can learn from Aaron here are simple. We must not let our faith fall to peer and social pressure. Don't worry about being labeled as weird or strange. Jesus was labeled the same way when He was here. Christians do not belong to this world. We are foreigners here. Trying to fit into the world's mold is contrary to what God clearly tells us.

In his book, *Hide or Seek*, James Dobson cites a study conducted by Ruth W. Berenda and her associates. They carried out an interesting experiment with teenagers designed to show how a person handled group pressure. The plan was simple. They brought groups of ten adolescents into a room for a test. Subsequently, each group of ten was instructed to raise their hands when the teacher pointed to the longest line on three separate charts. What one person in the group did not know was that nine of the others in the room had been instructed ahead of time to vote for the second-longest line.

Regardless of the instructions they heard, once they were all together in the group, the nine were not to vote for the longest line, but rather vote for the next-to-longest line.

The desire of the psychologist was to determine how one person reacted when completely surrounded by a large number of people who obviously stood against what was true.

The experiment began with nine teenagers voting for the wrong line. The stooge would typically glance around, frown in confusion, and slip his hand up with the group. The instructions were repeated, and the next card was raised. Time after time, the self-conscious stooge would sit there saying a short line is longer than a long line, simply because he lacked the courage to challenge the group. This remarkable conformity occurred in about 75% of the cases and was true of small children and high school students as well. Berenda concluded that, "Some people had rather be President than right" which is certainly an accurate assessment.[16]

Fan the Flame

Have you ever felt you were being pressured to do something you feel God wouldn't want you to do? If you have, did you give in to your peers? What were the consequences? How did you feel afterwards?

_____

_____

_____

_____

_____

_____

_____

Aaron's making of the golden calf and the big party that followed was completely against the laws God had given the people. Severe consequences resulted from it. Read the entire chapter of Exodus 32 and see how God felt about their disobedience.

_____

_____

_____

16 • Dobson, J. C. (1982). *Hide or seek: How to build self-esteem in your child.* Fleming H. Revell Co.

_____

_____

_____

_____

_____

_____

_____

We see where God was so angry with the people He threatened to kill all of them and make a nation from Moses's descendants. Have you ever thought that God can get angry at us? It certainly should make you pause before making decisions that go against God. Don't think that God will allow your sin to go unpunished just because you haven't witnessed his punishment firsthand. The people of Israel had just experienced a "high" having heard from God directly. Yet they gave up waiting on God to act and took matters into their own hands. Satan often attacks after a spiritual high. Expect it and be on guard against him.

You may say that God loves you and would never harm you. That is true. God loves you completely. You are His child if you have given your life over to Him. But God is also the final judge of our life. Just because we are His children doesn't mean that our wrongdoings will go unpunished. Remember that when peer pressure is staring you in the face.

Jadon
The Man of God,
What is Truth?

I Kings 13

I heard a story that really impacted me. It seems a young man fell in love with a woman about his age. They both truly loved each other and wanted to get married but neither had a job or money. The man loved to farm. He asked a wealthy man if he could rent a couple acres of his farm to try to make some money. The wealthy man agreed, and the man and woman soon had enough money to get married. God blessed them so much that they were eventually able to purchase the land they were farming from the wealthy man. In short time, they had earned enough to buy even more land and God blessed them tremendously with bumper crops. They built a house on the land and then decided to have kids to add to their family. In time, they had two lovely children. They were extremely blessed, and their home was a very happy one.

But one dark and rainy night, when the husband and wife were going out to dinner, they were involved in an accident in which both died instantly. The children were safe at home when this happened. With their parents gone, who would care for them? Both the husband and wife had no other siblings, and both sets of parents were also dead. There was only one elderly cousin who was found and told the children that they would live with her and help her. However, it was discovered that neither the husband nor the wife had any insurance or will and there was no money to be had. The state court became involved and declared the property belonged to the state, not the children. A public auction was held shortly thereafter. Strangers came and bought everything including the land, the house, everything! The children were then placed in the care of the State. The elderly cousin received nothing. The children received nothing. The State became the beneficiary of everything by law.

Now let me ask some questions? What is the eighth commandment? It reads, "You shall not steal." Did the State steal from the family? Do you think this is right? It is legal, but is it ethical?

This reminds me of a famous Bible story involving the evil king Ahab and a man named Naboth.

I Kings 21:1-16 (ESV)

Now Naboth the Jezreelite had a vineyard in Jezreel, beside the palace of Ahab king of Samaria. And after this Ahab said to Naboth, "Give me your vineyard, that I may have it for a vegetable garden, because it is near my house, and I will give you a better vineyard for it; or, if it seems good to you, I will give you its value in money." But Naboth said to Ahab, "The LORD forbid that I should give you the inheritance of my fathers." And Ahab went into his house vexed and sullen because of what Naboth the Jezreelite had said to him, for he had said, "I will not give you the inheritance of my fathers." And he lay down on his bed and turned away his face and would eat no food.

But Jezebel his wife came to him and said to him, "Why is your spirit so vexed that you eat no food?" And he said to her, "Because I spoke to Naboth the Jezreelite and said to him, 'Give me your vineyard for money, or else, if it please you, I will give you another vineyard for it.' And he answered, 'I will not give you my vineyard.'" And Jezebel his wife said to him, "Do you now govern Israel? Arise and eat bread and let your heart be cheerful; I will give you the vineyard of Naboth the Jezreelite."

So she wrote letters in Ahab's name and sealed them with his seal, and she sent the letters to the elders and the leaders who lived with Naboth in his city. And she wrote in the letters, "Proclaim a fast, and set Naboth at the head of the people. And set two worthless men opposite him, and let them bring a charge against him, saying, 'You have cursed God and the king.' Then take him out and stone him to death." And the men of his city, the elders and the leaders who lived in his city, did as Jezebel had sent word to them. As it was written in the letters that she had sent to them, they proclaimed a fast and set Naboth at the head of the people. And the two worthless men came in and sat opposite him. And the worthless men brought a charge against Naboth in the presence of the people, saying, "Naboth cursed God and the king." So they took him outside the city and stoned him to death with stones. Then they sent to Jezebel, saying, "Naboth has been stoned; he is dead."

As soon as Jezebel heard that Naboth had been stoned and was dead, Jezebel said to Ahab, "Arise, take possession of the vineyard of Naboth the Jezreelite, which he refused to give you for money, for Naboth is not alive, but dead." And as soon as Ahab heard that Naboth was dead, Ahab arose to go down to the vineyard of Naboth the Jezreelite, to take possession of it.

Many know this Bible story and it is frequently used for teaching how evil Ahab and Jezebel were. Evidently, Ahab and Jezebel stole the land. But did they?

The story I shared with you about the farmers is very similar. The government set up laws to establish the beneficiary. Did you note that Jezebel did the same thing? She followed the protocols of the day and had the law passed legally. Note in verse 8:

So she wrote letters in Ahab's name and sealed them with his seal, and she sent the letters to the elders and the leaders who lived with Naboth in his city.

I hate to admit it, but she did it according to the law.

Now let's return to the question, "Is what happened to the farmers right, or was it breaking the law?"

Here are some other questions. Is the government capable of declaring what is truth? If a government writes laws contrary to the laws of God found in His Word, is that ethical? Does the Word of God have any influence, emphasis, power, and prominence today in lawmaking? Or does the Word of God need to be changed due to cultural changes over time?

That story is a tough one for some people who might believe that God's Word is not absolute truth or that it might be voided due to cultural differences and time. But I strongly believe that the same God who created the world is the same yesterday, today and tomorrow! It is interesting when looking at the founding of the United States that the Founders cited twenty-seven biblical violations when the Declaration of Independence was penned. Even James Madison, the Father of the U.S. Constitution, included many biblical principles when writing that document. Today, some say that our Constitution is no longer binding. They say that it needs to be rewritten. But here I digress.

Let's examine a character God has placed in His Word that illustrates the point that laws can be wrong, even if signed by a king. The man in I Kings 13 is referred to as a "man of God came out of Judah." No name is associated with him in the Bible, but the ancient Jewish historian Josephus gives his name as Jadon. Whether that was his true name or not is not the issue here. We will refer to this prophet as Jadon to simplify the story. Since this story is not a well-known Bible story, let's read it and learn about this minor character.

I Kings 13:1-32 (ESV)
And behold, a man of God came out of Judah by the word
of the LORD to Bethel. Jeroboam was standing by the altar
to make offerings. And the man cried against the altar by
the word of the LORD and said, "O altar, altar, thus says the
LORD: 'Behold, a son shall be born to the house of David,

Josiah by name, and he shall sacrifice on you the priests of the high places who make offerings on you, and human bones shall be burned on you.'" And he gave a sign the same day, saying, "This is the sign that the LORD has spoken: 'Behold, the altar shall be torn down, and the ashes that are on it shall be poured out.'" And when the king heard the saying of the man of God, which he cried against the altar at Bethel, Jeroboam stretched out his hand from the altar, saying, "Seize him." And his hand, which he stretched out against him, dried up, so that he could not draw it back to himself. The altar also was torn down, and the ashes poured out from the altar, according to the sign that the man of God had given by the word of the LORD. And the king said to the man of God, "Entreat now the favor of the LORD your God, and pray for me, that my hand may be restored to me." And the man of God entreated the LORD, and the king's hand was restored to him and became as it was before. And the king said to the man of God, "Come home with me, and refresh yourself, and I will give you a reward." And the man of God said to the king, "If you give me half your house, I will not go in with you. And I will not eat bread or drink water in this place, for so was it commanded me by the word of the LORD, saying, 'You shall neither eat bread nor drink water nor return by the way that you came.'" So he went another way and did not return by the way that he came to Bethel.

Now an old prophet lived in Bethel. And his sons came and told him all that the man of God had done that day in Bethel. They also told to their father the words that he had spoken to the king. And their father said to them, "Which way did he go?" And his sons showed him the way that the man of God who came from Judah had gone. And he said to his sons, "Saddle the donkey for me." So they saddled the donkey for him and he mounted it. And he went after the man of God and found him sitting under an oak. And he said to him, "Are you the man of God who came from Judah?" And he said, "I am." Then he said to him, "Come home with me and eat bread." And he said, "I may not return with you, or go in with *you, neither will I eat bread nor drink water with you in this place, for it was said to me by the word of the LORD, 'You shall neither eat bread nor drink water there, nor return by the way that you came.'" And he said to him, "I also am a prophet as you are, and an angel spoke to me by the word of the LORD, saying, 'Bring him back with you into your house that he may eat bread and drink water.'" But he lied to him. So he went back with him and ate bread in his house and drank water.*

And as they sat at the table, the word of the LORD came to the prophet who had brought him back. And he cried to the man of God who came from Judah, "Thus says the LORD, 'Because you have disobeyed the word of the LORD and have not kept the command that the LORD your God commanded you, but have come back and have eaten bread and drunk water in the place of which he said to you, "Eat no bread and drink no water," your body shall not come to the tomb of your fathers.'" And after he had eaten bread and drunk, he saddled the donkey for the prophet whom he had brought back. And as he went away a lion met him on the road and killed him. And his body was thrown in the road, and the donkey stood beside it; the lion also stood beside the body. And behold, men passed by and saw the body thrown in the road and the lion standing by the body. And they came and told it in the city where the old prophet lived.

And when the prophet who had brought him back from the way heard of it, he said, "It is the man of God who disobeyed the word of the LORD; therefore the LORD has given him to the lion, which has torn him and killed him, according to the word that the LORD spoke to him." And he said to his sons, "Saddle the donkey for me." And they saddled it. And he went and found his body thrown in the road, and the donkey and the lion standing beside the body. The lion had not eaten the body or torn the donkey. And the prophet took up the body of the man of God and laid it on the donkey and brought it back to the city to mourn and to bury him. And he laid the body in his own grave. And they mourned over him, saying,

*"Alas, my brother!" And after he had buried him, he said
to his sons, "When I die, bury me in the grave in which the
man of God is buried; lay my bones beside his bones. For the
saying that he called out by the word of the Lord against the
altar in Bethel and against all the houses of the high places
that are in the cities of Samaria shall surely come to pass."*

The land of Israel that David built up had separated during the beginning of his grandson Rehoboam's reign. The southern two tribes, Judah and Benjamin, had remained loyal to David's lineage, but the ten northern tribes had disassociated themselves and formed a new "Israel" with Jeroboam as their king. He was not a good king. In the town of Bethel, he constructed a golden calf idol to be a representation of EL (a name of God) or YHWH (Yahweh), thus sinning gravely and leading the people into idol worship by combining YHWH with Baal (the god of the Canaanites) and Asherah (the immoral god of the Phoenicians).

Jeroboam chose to continue the festivals and holidays that were described by Moses in the Torah, but he chose his own people to be priests and prophets. This was contrary to God's laws, which stated that priests must be from the tribe of Levi. Jeroboam was leading the new Israel into a sinful and evil direction; however, God sent a prophet from Judah to give him an ultimatum. Josephus calls him Jadon.

Jadon appears on the scene at a festival in Bethel where Jeroboam had just dedicated the new golden calf idol on a new altar. Jadon approaches Jeroboam and proclaims God's Word to him.

I Kings 13:1-3 (GW)
*A man of God from Judah had come to Bethel. When he
arrived, Jeroboam was standing at the altar to offer a
sacrifice. By a command of the Lord, this man condemned
the altar. "Altar, altar! This is what the Lord says: There
will be a son born in David's family line. His name will be
Josiah. Here on you Josiah will sacrifice the priests from the
illegal worship sites who offer sacrifices on you. Human
bones will be burned on you." That day the man of God*

[also] gave [them] a miraculous sign, saying, "This is the
sign that the Lord will give you: You will see the altar torn
apart. The ashes on it will be poured [on the ground]."

Jadon called out the King for his sin in front of all his subjects. That takes guts! To prove that what he said came from God Himself and was not his own feelings, he stated that a miracle would show this to be true. Not only that, but he foretold of a future king named Josiah who would defile that new unholy altar, an event that did happen later. Scholars believe that Jeroboam built the altar around 930 B.C. and that King Josiah fulfilled that prophecy around 600 B.C. Jadon foretold the event over 200 years before it happened. But look at how Jeroboam reacts.

I Kings 13:4-5 (GW)
When King Jeroboam heard the man of God condemning
the altar in Bethel, he pointed to the man across the altar.
"Arrest him," he said. But the arm that he used to point
to the man of God was paralyzed so that he couldn't pull
it back. The altar was torn apart, and the ashes from the
altar were poured [on the ground]. This was the miraculous
sign the man of God performed at the Lord's command.

Let's examine this event in another word-for-word translation.

I Kings 13:4 (NASB, 1977)
Now it came about when the king heard the saying of the
man of God, which he cried against the altar in Bethel, that
Jeroboam stretched out his hand from the altar, saying,
"Seize him." But his hand which he stretched out against
him dried up, so that he could not draw it back to himself.

What happened to his arm and hand? The Hebrew word describing what happened is the word שֵׁבֵי **yabesh**, meaning to "wither." What this refers to is a bit of a mystery, but it appears that it died. The *Bible Background Commentary* describes this condition this way.

Most interpreters have identified this physical condition
as resulting from some source of hemorrhage or clot, but

these conditions do not explain why the arm remained extended. The latter has been described as a condition today termed "cataplexy" (a shock to the nervous system that causes muscle rigidity).

Can you imagine being there when this happened? It would surely send chills up your spine to hear Jadon speak and then see Jeroboam's arm react like that.

Let me pause for a moment and show you something interesting. Miracles do happen by God's power. If one examines the miracles in the Bible, one will see that miracles usually follow as proof that God has spoken through a person. They are not done for entertainment, but to prove that God's Word is true. This miracle occurred to prove the Word of God.

Changing God's laws and creating a new religion spelled doom for Jeroboam. They were both major sins in God's eyes. Jeroboam realized this at once. I think anyone would realize this considering what God did through this prophet. It impacted Jeroboam enough for him to call out to the prophet for help.

I Kings 13:6 (GW)
Then the king asked the man of God, "Please make an appeal to the LORD your God, and pray for me so that I can use my arm again." So the man of God made an appeal to the LORD, and the king was able to use his arm again, as he had earlier.

Don't you find it amazing that God would so easily heal him despite his sin? Notice, too, that Jeroboam recognized that Jadon was a true man of God, unlike the ones he chose to be prophets. Because of this experience, Jeroboam wanted to get the true prophet to stay with him.

Most Bible scholars agree that Jeroboam was not repentant about trying to establish a new religion in Israel. Most feel that he was attempting to bribe Jadon to gain his favor. We can see from future events that Jeroboam did not change his ways.

Jadon responded that he was not allowed to eat or drink anything on his journey nor even to stay in Israel, but to go home a different route as soon as possible. This was a statement that Israel was polluted with sin and its new religion was contaminated.

I Kings 13:7-10 (GW)

*The king told the man of God, "Come home with me;
have something to eat and drink, and I will give you a
gift." The man of God told the king, "Even if you gave me
half of your palace, I would never go with you to eat or
drink there. When the LORD spoke to me, he commanded
me not to eat or drink or go back on the same road
I took." So the man of God left on another road and
didn't go back on the road he had taken to Bethel.*

Jadon had heard God speak. He had heard His Word. It was true to him, and he would not alter it in any way to fit his own desires or needs.

After refusing King Jeroboam's offer, he set out for home thinking his mission was accomplished. However, something else was happening in Bethel.

I Kings 13:11-13 (GW)

*An old prophet was living in Bethel. His sons told him
everything the man of God did in Bethel that day and the
exact words he had spoken to the king. When they told their
father, he said to them, "Which road did he take?" (His sons
had seen which road the man of God from Judah had taken.)
The old prophet told his sons, "Saddle the donkey for me."
After they had saddled the donkey for him, he got on it.*

Another unnamed prophet appeared on the stage. We do not have any information about him nor is his name found in Scripture, but Josephus gives us a bit of his character.

*Now there was a certain wicked man in that city, who was
a false prophet, whom Jeroboam had in great esteem...[17]*

---

17 • Josephus, Flavius, and Whiston, William (1737). Anitquities of the Jews - Book VIII Ch 9 par 1. In *The Genuine Works of Flavius Josephus the Jewish Historian.*

Apparently, this man was no prophet of the Lord's because he was living in Bethel, and he did not appear to be doing anything about Jeroboam's new religious reforms. Instead, he was a deceiver of the truth. He sought out Jadon, who was traveling home as per God's instructions, but who was undoubtedly famished.

I Kings 13:14-15 (GW)

He went after the man of God and found him sitting under an oak tree. The old prophet asked him, "Are you the man of God who came from Judah?" "Yes," he answered. "Come home with me, and eat a meal," the old prophet replied.

This seems innocent enough but remember, God's Word was for Jadon not to indulge in anything in that spiritually polluted kingdom.

Jadon again spoke the truth from God's Word.

I Kings 13:16-17 (GW)

The man of God said, "I'm not allowed to go back with you. I'm not allowed to eat or drink with you. When the LORD spoke to me, he told me not to eat or drink there or go back on the road I took to get there."

The deceiver lied and unwittingly set a trap for Jadon.

I Kings 13:18-19 (GW)

The old prophet said, "I'm also a prophet, like you. An angel spoke the word of the LORD to me. He said, 'Bring him home with you so that he may have something to eat and drink.'" (But the old prophet was lying.) The man of God went back with him and ate and drank in his home.

Jadon compromised God's Word; he broke God's law. He knew what he had been told by God, but for some reason chose to believe that God's Word did not apply at that time. Did you catch that? Read that sentence again slowly and let it sink in. This is the same problem we see today. In a July 2005 issue of *Focus on the Family's—TruU Pamphlet*, the following is noted:

Truth is relative. It's whatever works for you....Christianity's for the weak minded. Faith and reason don't mix. "Christian intellectual?" That's an oxymoron. Recognize these beliefs? How will [young people] respond?

Statistics show that as many as 50% of young people lose their faith in college. Why? Because they have no idea why they believe what they believe, and they have no ability to defend their beliefs. They're taken captive by ideas they aren't prepared for.

Sound familiar? Those seeking to impose or justify their own selfish ambitions often distort the truth. What is truth? Pilate asked that same question of Jesus in 30 A.D. The only thing in this universe that is true is God. He is it! He created all the laws of science and matter. He spoke and, since He is the ultimate of holiness, He cannot lie. Everything that comes out of His mouth is truth! God is truth! God does not change. He is the same yesterday, today and tomorrow. To alter the truth is to ensure God's wrath. Look how the story plays out.

I Kings 13:20-22 (GW)
When they were sitting at the table, the Lord spoke his word to the old prophet who had brought back the man of God. The Lord also called to the man of God. He said, "This is what the Lord says: You rebelled against the words from the Lord's mouth and didn't obey the command that the Lord your God gave you. You came back, ate, and drank at this place about which he told you, 'Don't eat or drink there.' That is why your dead body will not be allowed to be placed in the tomb of your ancestors."

God's Word does not compromise the truth. Jadon was obviously hungry, thirsty, and tired. He knew the specific orders from God, but he chose to believe that His Word did not carry any weight then. He talked himself into distorting the truth.

How many today search for a compromised "truth" because they do not like God's Truth? How many today seek a church with a pastor who preaches lies and passes it off as God's Word? This has become an epidemic in our world today!

For Jadon, the consequences were severe!

I Kings 13:23-24 (GW)
After the old prophet had something to eat and drink, he saddled the donkey for the prophet whom he had brought back. The man of God left. A lion found him [as he traveled] on the road and killed him. His dead body was thrown on the road. The donkey and the lion were standing by the body.

If we try to figure out why God was so severe with Jadon and not the lying prophet who said that he got a message from an angel, we will be left wondering. The account does have a lesson for us, though. God will deal more strictly with those who are in His service than those worldly people who are not. We who are called by God to serve Him will be held more accountable than others.

Let's summarize Jadon's character. The following were his strengths and accomplishments: First, he was a man who had the special honor to serve God in Israel. Second, he was given God's Word to proclaim. Third, he was an instrument used by God to conduct miracles.

As to his weaknesses and mistakes, we read that first, he compromised the truth of God; second, he did not hold that God's Word is unchanging; third, he let his own personal desires supersede God's Word. He heard a message supposedly from a man who claimed to have received it from an angel and jumped at the chance to believe the lie all the while knowing deep down what God had told him.

Too often I have had discussions about the reality of truth, if it even exists today. The disturbing thing is that many times the people asking this question are Christian youth. These people are already saved by grace but are very confused by what they are taught in schools and sometimes by their church leaders. I have had young men who tried to convince me that what the

Bible calls sins are really not sins today because the Bible was written for an ancient Israel and not a post-modern America. Sometimes I have not been able to teach them that those abominations to God in the ancient days are still an abomination to Him today. God did not mellow about sin. Sin is still an unholy article that cannot be in His presence, for He is a holy God. Jesus told us what sin was, and that hasn't mellowed or changed with time. There is a truth our Holy God spoke, and it does not change with time!

I had just finished speaking at an event explaining this very thing. A couple of young men approached and stated that they did not believe in absolute truth; it is relative to an individual person. Another said he believed that there are many forms of truth; therefore, a person can make anything true. I asked them if they ever used mouthwash. This startled them a bit. I asked them if they ever used an oil product like WD-40® as mouthwash. They both replied negatively, thinking I was making a joke. I asked them that if a person stated as truth that WD-40® was mouthwash, would it hurt a person who used it in that fashion? As they stood there perplexed, I continued by asking what would happen if someone stated that Tylenol was candy? If they ate a whole bottle, thinking the analgesic pain-reliever was a harmless candy, did they think that their truth, insisting that it was candy, would not harm them? They thought for a bit and then asked where absolute truth could be found. I picked up my Bible and told them that it was right here.

Fan the Flame

Jadon was a prophet of God sent by God to give King Jeroboam a message. The king had set up his own pseudo-religion against the rules and regulations given by God to Moses in the book of Exodus. Exodus was written between 1450 – 1400 B.C. King Jeroboam set up his altar and priestly system in the north after the country split apart. His altar was built in the 9th Century (900 – 801 B.C.) – around 600 years later. Did God's Word evolve over the centuries as those in our current society believe? Absolutely not! Jadon's message told of the destruction of King Jeroboam's altar saying that the worship sites were illegal. And it was destroyed (II Kings 23:15-17). Time didn't change God's laws. God didn't change His mind. In fact, Malachi 3:6 states: "For I the LORD do not change." And centuries later in the book of Hebrews it again states that God doesn't change. "Jesus Christ is the same yesterday and today and forever."(Hebrews 13:8)

What about you? Do you believe what God said so long ago is true and relevant for today? If not, who or what is causing you to believe the Bible and God's Word aren't relevant? This is vital to your spiritual growth. You either believe the Bible in its entirety or you don't. Take a moment and think through your response then jot it down.

Take a look at I John 4:1-3. The Bible says in various places to test God. If you are unsure about Him, look for answers. Don't take anyone's word on the subject without checking into what God has to say about the matter. Does it contradict what God says in the Bible? Remember to read more than just a verse here and there. Read enough to get the context of what He is saying as just one verse or part of a verse can mislead you.

Whose word do you believe to be true? You must make that decision for yourself. If you don't know where to look in the Bible, I suggest two ways to find the answers. Look up topics in a concordance found in the back of most Bibles. You may have to get creative here and think of various words to look up. Another good source is a solid Christian believer such as a Bible-preaching minister or Bible teacher. But again, don't just take his word for it. Ask him to show you places in the Bible to look at. And remember, "And the Spirit is the one who testifies, because the Spirit is the truth." (I John 5:6)

Lot
Distracted From God by Complacency

Genesis 13:5-13 & 19:1-38

One of the most brilliant and intelligent people I have ever known was a friend of mine in high school whom we will call Jim. While I struggled to learn material in school, he would glean it easily. It just came naturally for him to not only learn, but to apply his knowledge. He was truly intelligent. Even so, we were very close friends.

Jim knew that there was something different about us besides our I.Q. He knew I was a Christian and that the desires of my life and heart were different than his. He also dealt with guilt and shame from his past, while he noticed I did not live with such problems. When he finally asked me about this, I told him that I repented and was forgiven by the grace of God and that Jesus is a major part of my life. In time Jim came with me to my church to see firsthand what my youth group was like and to try to figure out the Christian life. During that Sunday morning, the Spirit of God convicted him, and Jim repented and accepted Jesus Christ as his Lord and Savior. We were now brothers.

For the next couple of years, I helped Jim grow in his Christian life. I was amazed at how much God put into him. He already wanted to be a medical doctor, but then he felt compelled to be a missionary doctor to Africa. He had a deep desire to go there and set up a clinic in the remote areas where he could heal both body with medicine and the lost and hurting souls with Jesus Christ.

Jim quickly became one of the leaders of our youth at church. Together we started a visitation program, going into the south suburbs of Chicago and trying get young people to come to our youth group to meet Jesus. Jim would sometimes lead the devotional section of the adult Wednesday night prayer services.

Upon graduation from high school, Jim went to a Christian college to major in pre-med on his road to becoming a doctor/missionary. We would write to each other about our college experiences (as we were in two different schools in different states) and encourage each other in the Lord.

I graduated before Jim and moved out of the country to teach at a Christian school in the Bahamas. The night before I left Jim came over to see me. We sat outside and made a pledge to keep working for the Lord and to keep in touch with each other. Very soon afterwards, Jim and I lost touch and we never reconnected again. Little did I know that I would not see my best friend again. Years passed. Occasionally I would hear from other people from the old youth group, but no one ever seemed to mention Jim.

Nineteen years later, I finally tracked him down. I called him on the phone, and we had a peculiar conversation. I told him that I was heading to the mission field and leaving my career as a schoolteacher. He calmly replied that this sounded okay, but I noticed his tone was not cheerful. I asked him what he was doing with his life. He unenthusiastically replied he was doing fine; that he was making a lot of money working for a large pharmaceutical company. He mentioned that he had some patents and that his career was very successful. While he spoke, I noticed that the excitement that used to be in his voice was gone. When I asked him about his personal life, he replied that although he had married a girl he met in college, he didn't really love her. They had a few kids and then divorced. He had married another girl, but that, too, ended in divorce. He was now on his third marriage, but he was not happy with it either.

I asked him what was going on spiritually in his life. He depressingly said, "Not much." Quickly and with no details, he told me that his spiritual life died near the end of his senior year in college. He ended his commentary by stating that he wished he could regain that feeling he had as a teen in youth group, but that his career and success robbed him of it.

I pleaded for him to come back to God, but he strongly said, "I don't want to talk about that anymore!" Moments later we hung up.

Sometimes people can get on fire for God in their youth and then it seems that Satan comes along and snuffs out the flame. He does not do it alone. We allow him quite an arsenal to extinguish the flames of our spiritual fire. God gives us an example of such a situation in the book of Genesis. It concerns a nephew of Abraham named Lot. His story, like Jim's, began great but diminishes to the bog of despair and sadness.

We first encounter Lot when he leaves the blessings of residing with his uncle Abraham.

Genesis 13:5-13 (ESV)
And Lot, who went with Abram, also had flocks and herds and tents, so that the land could not support both of them dwelling together; for their possessions were so great that they could not dwell together, and there was strife between the herdsmen of Abram's livestock and the herdsmen of Lot's livestock. At that time the Canaanites and the Perizzites were dwelling in the land.

Then Abram said to Lot, "Let there be no strife between you and me, and between your herdsmen and my herdsmen, for we are kinsmen. Is not the whole land before you? Separate yourself from me. If you take the left hand, then I will go to the right, or if you take the right hand, then I will go to the left." And Lot lifted up his eyes and saw that the Jordan

Valley was well watered everywhere like the garden of the LORD, like the land of Egypt, in the direction of Zoar. (This was before the LORD destroyed Sodom and Gomorrah.) So Lot chose for himself all the Jordan Valley, and Lot journeyed east. Thus they separated from each other. Abram settled in the land of Canaan, while Lot settled among the cities of the valley and moved his tent as far as Sodom. Now the men of Sodom were wicked, great sinners against the LORD.

From this passage, we see a young Lot who had been tremendously blessed with possessions and a loving family. Due to quarrels between the workers, Abraham suggested that they put some space between their camps. Abraham offered Lot his choice of land. Sodom and Gomorrah were awfully enticing to Lot, so he chose that area.

Abraham was extremely wealthy from God's provisions, and he was content to continue to allow God to bless him by leading him to live where He wanted. Lot on the other hand, looked to the cities of Sodom and Gomorrah with all their enticements as the place he would find fulfillment.

I have always found it amazing how young people in general have such a desire to live in the big cities. Being raised on the south side of Chicago, I always had a desire to live away from such places. Even when I worked in Chicago at the John G. Shedd Aquarium I never wanted to move there with all of its man-made architecture and vice. However, most teens I have taught seem to relish this type of environment. (Please understand, I am not saying Chicago is Sodom or Gomorrah, but I know that vice and other enticements are very abundant there.) Lot was no different. Notice carefully verse twelve and where Lot made camp. It reads "Lot settled among the cities of the valley and moved his tent as far as Sodom."

At least Lot had the spiritual sense not to move directly into the cities but camped near them. To maintain his wealth, he needed the trade of the cities to grow financially. He had a good religious upbringing through his uncle Abraham and had spiritual common sense that seemed to override his desire to live in the city. That's good.

Not long afterwards we find Lot being kidnapped. But look where he was living when it happened.

Genesis 14:12 (ESV)
They [the kidnappers] also took Lot, the son of
Abram's brother, who was dwelling in Sodom,
and his possessions, and went their way.

Disaster befalls Lot. He is robbed and kidnapped. How could this have happened? Could it be that Lot has begun to compromise his standards and morals? We don't know. We do know that he was still wealthy but had indeed moved into the sinful city. Thankfully, Abraham chased after the bad guys and freed his nephew and his belongings (verse 16).

Fast forward about twenty-five years. Abraham had just been told by God and two angels that Sodom and Gomorrah were about to be obliterated from the face of the earth because of their sin. Abraham knew that his nephew was still living in So-dom and began pleading with God for his life and the life of his family (Chapter 18). We pick up the story in Genesis nineteen.

Genesis 19:1a (ESV)
The two angels came to Sodom in the evening,
and Lot was sitting in the gate of Sodom.

Observe where Lot is when the angels arrive. He was sitting in the city gate. God informed us about an important detail in Lot's life. In ancient times, the city gate was not just a doorway into and out of the city. It was a governmental place where legal is-sues were conducted. The gate was a large structure with many rooms and not just a door. Judges and city officials would sit in rooms constructed in the walls at the gate. It was a place to do business and have meetings.

The fact that Lot was sitting in the city gate indicates that he had risen to some importance in the civil affairs of the city. He met the two strangers there and invited them to his home for safety.

During the evening meal Lot's home was besieged by a group of men who exemplify the perverted nature of the now infamous city. They want to rape the "young men" who were actually angels sent by God to destroy the city.

Genesis 19:4-5 (GW)
Before they had gone to bed, all the young and old male citizens of Sodom surrounded the house. They called to Lot, "Where are the men who came to [stay with] you tonight? Bring them out to us so that we can have sex with them."

This sin went against the natural order God had created; He hated it. Judgment Day had come to Sodom and Gomorrah.

Lot tried to protect his guests and in doing so we can read how degraded he himself had become from living in the midst of this evil society. Listen to his solution to the danger.

Genesis 19:6-8 (GW)
Then Lot went outside and shut the door behind him. "Please, my friends, don't be so wicked," he said. "Look, I have two daughters who have never had sex. Why don't you let me bring them out to you? Do whatever you like with them. But don't do anything to these men, since I'm responsible for them."

Can you believe what this man is saying and offering? This shows us that he had compromised his relationship with God for the gains of living in Sodom. Friends, we must be careful not to become contaminated by the sinful nature that surrounds us. I am not saying that we should avoid such people. Oh, no! We are to be a light and ambassadors of Jesus to such people. We are to love people just as God loved us while we were still sinners.

What advantages could Lot have gained by living in Sodom? Many of these are temptations for families even today. First, it was beneficial for business exchanges in the city. Second, it was a place to advertise his wares. Third, it had many shops and markets which brought business success. Fourth, it was a place to find entertainment after working all day. Fifth, it no doubt gave him a feeling of power by being added to the civil counsel. Sixth, it yielded friendships for fun and relaxation. Seventh, it had popular schools for raising kids. Eighth, it helped with popularity. Ninth, it offered many indulging hobbies. Tenth, it would be a place to find a mate.

Let's face it. Those reasons can replace God in a person's heart today. Not all of them are bad, but I have seen them used by Satan to steal away the spiritual life of a young Christian. Now don't get me wrong. I am not saying that we need to devoid ourselves of such things and live out in the wilderness like a hermit. That was a popular notion during the Middle Ages, but it does not work. God does not want us to remove ourselves from society. He wants us to be the light and the salt there. He wants us to be His ambassadors to the world, but we must be very careful not to fall into Lot's predicament.

Thankfully, God did not allow Lot to use his virgin daughters as a sacrifice to these scoundrels. The angels pulled him inside and protected his family from those perverts. They blinded the evil men and then told Lot to tell his family to leave the city.

Genesis 19:12-14 (ESV)
Then the men said to Lot, "Have you anyone else here? Sons-in-law, sons, daughters, or anyone you have in the city, bring them out of the place. For we are about to destroy this place, because the outcry against its people has become great before the LORD, and the LORD has sent us to destroy it." So Lot went out and said to his sons-in-law, who were to marry his daughters, "Up! Get out of this place, for the LORD is about to destroy the city." But he seemed to his sons-in-law to be jesting.

After this, we see Lot losing everything he had gained in that city, for he lingered instead of running. Wealth, possessions, prestige, and popularity are hard items for some people to sacrifice to God.

Genesis 19:15-16 (ESV)
*As morning dawned, the angels urged Lot, saying, "Up!
Take your wife and your two daughters who are here, lest
you be swept away in the punishment of the city." But he
lingered. So the men seized him and his wife and his two
daughters by the hand, the LORD being merciful to him,
and they brought him out and set him outside the city.*

Lot couldn't seem to let go of his possessions, position, friends, and other enticements of the city. However, for the sake of a promise to Abraham, God had His angels force them out of the city—just him, his wife and two daughters. Though Lot tried to save others, none believed him. With Lot and his family safely out of the way, God destroyed the cities of Sodom and Gomorrah.

On a side note, some skeptics and critics of the Bible say that the destruction of Sodom is a fairytale. But recent archaeological evidence from excavations performed by Dr. Steven Collins and others suggest that it may have been located at Tall el-Hammam in Jordan. Some of the evidence attesting to this is an ash layer over one meter thick, foundations and floors of buildings that have been scorched by high heat, dozens of pottery sherds that appear melted and some turned into a glass—requiring heat, in excess of over 2,000F, far beyond that of ancient kilns at the time of the Middle Bronze Age (2000–1600 B.C.). (*tallelhammam.com*)

As the catastrophic events were being played out and the cities were destroyed, Lot's wife was killed by God for her disobedience.

Genesis 19:26 (ESV)
*But Lot's wife, behind him, looked back,
and she became a pillar of salt.*

This punishment has often puzzled readers. The Hebrew term for "looked" found here is נָבַט **nabat**, which means to scan, or look intently at with regards of pleasure, favor, or care. It is likely that Lot's wife was looking back not to see the destruction but had turned around to look intently at the city she called home and all of its possessions that she was leaving behind. This, of course, was sinful as she was commanded by God to not even glance back to the city He was going to destroy.

Lot had lost his wife, besides his future sons-in-law, and all his possessions. He was left alone with only his two daughters. But again, we see how far Lot's relationship with God has fallen.

Genesis 19:30-36 (GW)

Lot left Zoar because he was afraid to stay there. He and his two daughters settled in the mountains where they lived in a cave. The older daughter said to the younger one, "Our father is old. No men are here. We can't get married as other people do. Let's give our father wine to drink. Then we'll go to bed with him so that we'll be able to preserve our family line through our father." That night they gave their father wine to drink. Then the older one went to bed with her father. He didn't know when she came to bed or when she got up. The next day the older daughter said to the younger one, "I did it! Last night I went to bed with my father. Let's give him wine to drink again tonight. Then you go to bed with him so that we'll be able to preserve our family line through our father." That night they gave their father wine to drink again. Then the younger one went to bed with him. He didn't know when she came to bed or when she got up. So Lot's two daughters became pregnant by their father.

Poor Lot. This passage shows us not only how far he had fallen, but also what a poor job he did at raising his own family. Listen men; don't think for a moment that raising a family without being a godly, fatherly influence is acceptable. Young girls in particular need to see the Father God in you. You are His representative and model for them. Treat and love them the same way God loves you and show it often. Be there for them and guide them in a deep, loving relationship.

The story of Lot ends here in Scripture. What an epitaph to his life. But God put his story in the Bible to teach us. He shows us that the advantages of having malls, possessions, friends, prestige, sports, hobbies, jobs, entertainment, and even the place we live can be disadvantages if Satan uses them as a weapon to diminish our relationship with God. Be wary of Satan's weapons. Don't let Satan steal your heart away from God. Be on your guard, for Satan can attack you with very subtle things.

An unsuspecting fly was beginning to sense a sweet, sugary smell in the air as it flew over a bog. Flying in the direction of its origin, the fly noticed many bright red droplets on small leaves of plants. Curious, and looking for a meal, the fly landed near the numerous pads of leaves covered with the red drops. He smelled a droplet. It smelled sweet like sugar. Looking around for predators, the fly saw none. These droplets looked delicious, and it seemed safe, so he lapped up the juice of one single droplet. It tasted as he thought – delicious. Ever cautious, the fly scanned the area for predators. Everything seemed safe to him, so he lapped up another droplet. Again, he searched for predators and saw none, so he walked upon the small pad-like leaves and continued to lap up the sugary substance. After consuming one group of droplets, he found that he just craved more and more. He would stop every few moments to look for a frog, salamander, or spider, but saw none. He thought, I have really found paradise, and it is all mine.

As the minutes passed by, the fly was busy consuming its sugary meal. He never saw any predators and so continued to walk around the sugary restaurant where he was sitting. Unbeknownst to the fly, the leaves of the plant he was sitting upon were moving but moving at a rate he never noticed.

In his gluttony, the sugary droplets were hindering his walking around on the plant. He was finding it harder and harder to move, but it didn't scare him as the food was so delicious. He also noticed that the leaves had moved up around him and it almost seemed to him that the plant was trying to capture him. But he was a fly, and this was just a plant, so he was not too alarmed by this discovery as the droplets tasted so good.

After engorging himself on the droplets, he tried to fly away. Suddenly the fly realized he was stuck. The sugar droplets were also very sticky, and the pad-like leaves of the plant were now encompassing him. The more he squirmed the more he was coated with the sticky, sugary droplets. He was caught by the beautiful and harmless looking plant, which pressed on his body and began secreting chemicals which not only killed him but digested him. The fly had landed on a cap sundew in a bog, an insectivorous or sometimes called a carnivorous plant that tempts insects with sweet, red drops of sugar on it leaves and then devours it to supply chemicals it cannot obtain in the nutrient poor soil of a bog.

Fan the Flame

Has there been a time of tension within your family that caused you to break away from them?

_____

_____

_____

_____

_____

_____

_____

What do you think caused it?

_____

_____

_____

_____

_____

_____

_____

Has there been a time you felt separated from God?

What do you think caused it?

We all live in an area and know people who accept ungodly things into their lives. What steps can you take to keep away from the temptations around you that have/could cause a break between you and God?

Gehazi
When Priorities Become a Problem

II Kings 5: 19-27

I once had an interesting student who enrolled in my seventh-grade science class. At the beginning of that school year, he came to me and said that he did not do homework. Instead, he wanted to do extra credit. When I questioned him about the necessity of doing the assigned work over unassigned work, he simply replied that his dad would support his decision. I called the home and asked the father to come and see me about his son's work.

A few days later, the three of us met and he asked me what this was all about. I told him that his son had told me that he would not do any homework this year in my class and would only do extra credit. I also informed him that his son was living up to his promise; he had not turned in one assignment! I told the father that I needed his help by taking responsibility for his son completing the work assigned, not just the extra credit. The father became uneasy before informing me that the two of them had, indeed, concocted the plan. He said he had succeeded in life without science and if he could do it, his son could too. In short, he told me that what I was trying to teach his son was utterly worthless and a waste of his son's time and efforts. He then leaned back in his chair and studied my face to see if his cutting remarks had the impact he had hoped for.

I sat there literally stunned! I felt that not only my profession had been violated by this man and his son but myself too. Then a wicked grin spread across his face. He turned and winked at his grinning son.

I was determined not to let this man or his son feel any sort of victory. I thought quickly and asked him what he did for a living. He obviously wasn't expecting this question. He slumped a little in his chair as he described his low-skilled job at a factory, but he added at the end of his description that science was not something he used in his job or life. I asked him if he was happy with his choice of career. He admitted to me that he was not, but he would soon not have to work there. Surprised, I asked him why, and his response floored me. He said that in a few years his son would be out of school and playing in the NBA, making millions. He could then retire and live off his son's earnings. As he said this, his son beamed a smile as big as a watermelon. He said the only subject this school could help his son with was basketball in gym class. He defiantly stated, "The important thing in my son's education at this school is to get that orange ball in that hoop!"

I now saw that I had to educate two individuals who did not want to learn. I tried to assure him that many parents and students had such dreams across the country, but very few people made it to the NBA. I asked him what he thought his son would do if he didn't make it to the NBA. What could he fall back on? He replied, "He will make it! I will see to it!"

Unfortunately for this family, this boy never made it to the NBA. He was not even the star player on the team we had at that school. He struggled all through school that year because dad had driven him with misplaced life priorities.

Having the wrong priorities in life can get a person into real trouble. This includes your relationship with God. We are going to examine a lesser-known biblical character who teaches us the consequences of getting our priorities out of correct sequence with God. His name is Gehazi, the servant of the great prophet Elisha.

We first come upon Gehazi as he accompanied the prophet in II Kings 4:12-14 when Elisha asked him for input on how to honor a faithful family.

II Kings 4:14 (ESV)
And he said, "What then is to be done for her?"
Gehazi answered, "Well, she has no son,
and her husband is old."

Gehazi seemed to have a knack for giving this generous family a tremendous gift. In the ancient Jewish culture, to be childless indicated that the mother was not in good standing with the Lord. The neighbors would have looked down upon her. It was the lowest disgrace an honorable woman could have. I am impressed that Gehazi did not even consider a monetary reward. He went to her heart and soul for the greatest honor she could hope for. And we see by her response in verse 16 that she had given up this hope and dream.

So, three cheers for Gehazi and his suggestion in verse 14, which obviously the Lord wanted to do for her.

The story continues as Gehazi helped the family again while serving his master Elisha. The son, who Gehazi suggested would make a wonderful reward for the faithfulness of this family, had suddenly died. The mother was heartbroken and went herself to find Elisha. When she approached the two, Gehazi saw her in the distance and Elisha sent him to talk to her at a distance and find out what the trouble was about. She did not tell Gehazi but kept coming to finally fall at the feet of Elisha. Now we see a different Gehazi. He pushed her aside.

II Kings 4:27 (ESV)
And when she came to the mountain to the man of
God, she caught hold of his feet. And Gehazi came
to push her away. But the man of God said, "Leave
her alone, for she is in bitter distress, and the LORD
has hidden it from me and has not told me."

She did not tell Gehazi her problem but deceived him. His response was to send her away because he did not realize that she was in great distress from a broken heart. Fortunately for her, Elisha was indifferent to his servant and told him to leave her alone. Elisha had what we today call "people skills." He could relate with people and sense how to work with them. Gehazi obviously did not possess these skills. His pride was likely a bit damaged, and he wanted nothing to do with her.

Before getting the entire story, Elisha handed his staff to the youthful and hard-hearted servant Gehazi and sent him to heal the boy. Elisha thought the son was only sick, not dead.

II Kings 4:29 (ESV)
He said to Gehazi, "Tie up your garment and take my staff in your hand and go. If you meet anyone, do not greet him, and if anyone greets you, do not reply. And lay my staff on the face of the child."

Obviously Gehazi was unable to do anything because the boy was dead. Let's get an idea of how much time had elapsed. The family lived in Shunem, and Elisha was on Mount Carmel. The distance between them is almost thirty miles. Although less than an hour's drive today, in those days traveling by donkey over dirt roads meant days of travel. That boy was dead, really dead!

Gehazi returned to find Elisha and the woman on route to her home. When they arrived, Elisha went alone into the room with the dead child. Gehazi and the family were sitting outside wondering what was going to happen.

I can't help but wonder what Gehazi was thinking at this point. Here he had tried to dismiss the woman because she would not confide in him, then he traveled as quickly as possible to reach the child first, only to find he was unable to help despite the instructions. The child was still dead. Did he sit there wondering about his own faith? Did he wonder why he was shut out of the room while Elisha went in alone? Did he feel embarrassed that he was not in the room with his master? We are not told. In any case, the boy was raised back to life and Elisha shouted for Gehazi to come.

II Kings 4:36 (ESV)
Then he summoned Gehazi and said, "Call this
Shunammite." So he called her. And when she
came to him, he said, "Pick up your son."

Gehazi was the first to see the woman's son alive and had the honor of presenting the living child back to her. The awkward setting in the waiting room was gone and he was relieved to be a part of this miracle at last.

After this episode, Gehazi was able to witness his master perform many amazing miracles. Naaman, the commander of the Syrian army, came to Elisha's door seeking healing from his disease of leprosy. The Syrians, who were enemies of the Israelites, had invaded the land and taken captives away as slaves. As the story goes, when God healed Naaman, he rode back to Elisha and tried to give him a substantial reward in payment for his healing. Since God did the healing by grace alone and not for money, Elisha flatly refused these monetary rewards. However, Gehazi was watching and coveting in his heart. When Naaman finally realized that Elisha was not going to take any prizes, he departed for his own country with his wealth. Now let's pick up the story in the Bible.

II Kings 5:20-24 (ESV)
Gehazi, the servant of Elisha the man of God, said, "See, my
master has spared this Naaman the Syrian, in not accepting
from his hand what he brought. As the LORD lives, I will run
after him and get something from him." So Gehazi followed
Naaman. And when Naaman saw someone running after
him, he got down from the chariot to meet him and said, "Is
all well?" And he said, "All is well. My master has sent me to
say, 'There have just now come to me from the hill country of
Ephraim two young men of the sons of the prophets. Please
give them a talent of silver and two changes of clothing.'"

And Naaman said, "Be pleased to accept two talents." And he urged him and tied up two talents of silver in two bags, with two changes of clothing, and laid them on two of his servants. And they carried them before Gehazi. And when he came to the hill, he took them from their hand and put them in the house, and he sent the men away, and they departed

Gehazi had his priorities really mixed up. Let's examine what his life in ministry has been like thus far. First, he had been chosen to be a servant of the prophet Elisha. That was quite an honor in itself. Second, he had been witness to remarkable miracles and events to strengthen his faith in God. Third, he had been involved in a dynamic ministry that had helped others align their lives with God. Fourth, he had been a tool used by God to help perform miracles in ministry. Fifth, he had been present to fantastic teachings about God. Not many people were able to follow a major prophet around, learning from him first-hand. Sixth, he had had the privilege of serving God in the mission field.

After all this, Gehazi experienced a change in his life. His "sinful flesh" took over. He not only stole and lied, but because his focus was on himself and not on God, he made five sinful choices. First, he coveted the wealth that was presented to Elisha. It was not his to have, but his human nature overcame his desire to do God's will. Second, he flatly lied to Naaman for needs that did not exist. He distorted the truth for his own gain. Third, he exploited a new convert on the pretext of a religious nature. This was a very serious sin. To use a new convert in an unholy act while saying that you are serving God is a powerful sin. Fourth, he flatly lied to Elisha about being gone and what he did. That was amazing considering how close Elisha was to God. I wonder how he even thought he could fool Elisha, but he tried. Fifth, he destroyed God's image of healing by grace alone. That was probably the most serious result of his sin. Naaman left believing that God grants grace to people who turn to Him, but Gehazi changed the message to say that one must pay for God's grace. The truth came out, howerver, when he returned to Elisha after hiding his stash.

II Kings 5:25-27 (ESV)

He went in and stood before his master, and Elisha said to him, "Where have you been, Gehazi?" And he said, "Your servant went nowhere." But he said to him, "Did not my heart go when the man turned from his chariot to meet you? Was it a time to accept money and garments, olive orchards and vineyards, sheep and oxen, male servants and female servants? Therefore the leprosy of Naaman shall cling to you and to your descendants forever." So he went out from his presence a leper, like snow.

Why do we think that we can get away with sin? We know that God is present and watching, but it is like we say to ourselves, "I know I can do this without anyone but God seeing me, and I know He won't say a word." We intentionally mix up our priorities and deceive ourselves about the impact sin will make on our lives. We might get away with our sins for a moment, but they can eat away at our souls, driving us further away from God. We may put on a godly show to people around us, but deep inside, we are being eaten away as from a worm that wants to devour our soul and our relationship with God. Gehazi thought he had gotten away with the sin, but as sin usually does, it becomes public. Maybe not right away, but it does become public at sometime. In the meantime, it messes up our lives so much that we confess to the sin to alleviate the pain. I have yet to find a sin that has benefited a person in the long haul. You may be sitting there right now thinking that some sin you have done has rewarded you, but believe me, it will only bring trouble, despair, or even worse. Gehazi walked away with a consequence that would affect him for the rest of his life. No longer could he be involved in ministry, for he could not live in his home or even be with his family or friends. He was an outcast.

There are at least four things we can learn from Gehazi. First, keep your devotional times with God. Pray daily to keep your relationship strong and healthy. Communication is so important in a healthy relationship. Listen to God by reading His 66 love letters. Speak to Him often in prayer, telling Him what's on your mind, communicating as one best friend does to another. Second, while you are praying, don't forget to ask for help and protection from committing sins. When Jesus taught his disciples to pray, He said, "lead us not into temptation; but deliver us from evil" (Matthew 6:13). Third, have a friend hold you accountable. You cannot hold yourself accountable. Find a close friend whom you can confide with and help hold you close to God. Fourth, hold on tightly to your relationship with God. If Gehazi could be lead astray after witnessing all he had seen Elisha do, we all can be too.

The late Reverend Billy Graham often challenged young people and adults by saying, "What will you be like as a Christian ten years from now? Many will be walking with Christ and serving Him in various capacities around the world, but for others there will be a tragedy because ten years from now they will have lost their burning zeal and love for Christ. Not necessarily because they wanted to or because they set their heart in rebellion against God's will, but because they set their life by the world's agenda."[18]

William Barclay in his book, *The Gospel of Luke*, wrote,

> *It is possible to be a follower of Jesus without being a disciple; to be a camp follower without being a soldier of the king; to be a hanger-on in some great work without pulling one's weight. Once, someone was talking to a great scholar about a younger man. He said, "So and so tells me that he was one of your students." The teacher answered devastatingly, "He may have attended my lectures, but he was not one of my students." There is a world of difference between attending lectures and being a student. It is one of the supreme handicaps of the Church that in the Church there are so many distant followers of Jesus and so few real disciples.*[19]

---

18 • Heard at the Urbana Conference, 1984.

19 • Barclay, W. (1975). On Counting the Cost. *In The Gospel of Luke*. The Westminster Press.

Fan the Flame

What are your goals in life?

_____

_____

_____

_____

_____

_____

_____

What are your current priorities?

_____

_____

_____

_____

_____

_____

_____

Will these priorities help you achieve your goals? If not, are they worth keeping? If so, why?

_____

_____

_____

_____

_____

_____

_____

_____

Have you secretly done something wrong that later came out? What happened when it became known? Were the consequences worth it?

Can you hide anything from God? Read Psalm 139:7-12 and write down your interpretation of these verses.

Ehud

*Fitting in When Others
Think You're Weird*

Judges 3:12-30

The year was 1969. The place was Sunset Strip, California. The person was a strange young man named Arthur Blessitt. He was a minister to the hippies, druggies, and social outcasts of the times. He ran a "church" called His Place, a building often filled with runaways, stoned people, bikers, and misfits. But Arthur took Jesus literally when he said that it was not the healthy that needed a physician but those who were sick. Jesus didn't come to call the righteous but the sinners to repentance (Luke 5:30-31). So, Blessitt left his "normal" church and moved to Sunset Strip where there were a host of sinners and where grace could be distributed. He often quoted Romans 5:20 (KJV), "But where sin abounded, grace did much more abound." More than that, he felt compelled by God to craft a 40-pound cross and not only carry it across the U.S.A. but across most other countries in the world. In fact, Blessitt holds the world's longest walk record, and he is still going at age 83!

This guy was and is an oddball. He has been ridiculed, arrested, spit upon, beaten, and slandered. Even so, he says, "I forgive." In the 60s and 70s he wrote an autobiography, *Turned onto Jesus*, which describes a "hippie-like" individual with his psychedelic covered Bible and weird clothes.

One of the key events in this oddball's life that affected people all over the world occurred when he was preaching at a Jesus meeting in Midland, Texas, at the Chaparral Center. The meeting was called "Decision '84! Date: April 1-6". An oilman named George W. Bush was listening to Arthur speak on the radio as he felt uncomfortable attending the center himself. However, he had a friend of his call Arthur and set up a meeting as he felt compelled to talk with Arthur. They met the next day at a Midland restaurant. The following is taken from the published journal of Arthur Blessitt:

> *Jim Sale, who lived in Midland, was also in the oil business. He came to me and said "George W. Bush, the Vice President's son wants to meet you and talk about Jesus. He does not feel comfortable attending the meeting at the Chaparral Center but has been listening on the radio. Will you meet with him?" I agreed and we arranged a time to meet the next day.*

> *Jim and I walked into the room at the arranged time and Mr. George W. Bush got up to shake our hands. He already knew my Midland friend. Mr. Bush asked how I was enjoying Midland and how the meetings were going. He said he had been listening on the radio. I told him everything was wonderful and the response at the meeting and in the city was great.*

> *Then George W. Bush looked at me, direct in the eyes with a calm steady look and said, "Arthur, I did not feel comfortable attending the meeting, but I want to talk to you about how to know Jesus Christ and how to follow Him."*

> *I was quite shocked at his direct and sincere approach. Few people just bring up that type of subject themselves and especially within only two or three minutes of our meeting. I had been praying for him since last night when*

I heard he wanted to talk. My friend Jim and I had also prayed for Mr. Bush. Now I whispered a silent prayer, "Oh Jesus put your words in my mouth and lead him to understand and be saved."

I slowly leaned forward and lifted the Bible that was in my hand and began to speak.

"What is your relationship with Jesus?" I asked.

He replied, "I'm not sure."

"Let me ask you this question. If you died this moment, do you have the assurance you would go to heaven?"

"No," he replied.

"Then let me explain to you how you can have that assurance and know for sure that you are saved."

He replied, "I like that."

I then begin to share... how to know and follow Jesus.[20]

This well-documented meeting changed the life of one man who served as the President of the United States of America and is one of the most influential men in the world. Oddballs like Arthur Blessitt are often used by God to promote His plans. The Bible contains many oddballs used by God. Men like Elijah, John the Baptist, Paul, John, and Peter, just to name a few well-known eccentrics. In this series, we are examining some lesser-known ones. In this lesson we will meet a man called Ehud.

Ehud lived in Israel during a period of time before Israel had a king but were instead ruled by Judges. It was an up and down time for them as they wavered back and forth in their relationship with God. When they refused to follow God, He punished Israel by letting the surrounding nations (the nations that the Israelites were supposed to exterminate from the land) invade

20 • Blessitt, A. (1984, April 23). *Praying with George W. Bush.* blessitt.com. https://blessitt.com/praying-with-george-w-bush/

and make slaves of the Jews. When the Jews woke up and called out to God, He chose a Judge for them to relieve the oppression and lead them back to Himself. During one of those times of slavery, Moab had control of Israel. Moab originated from the descendants of Lot's incestuous sin with one of his daughters. The king of Moab was a man named Eglon, who was very, very fat.

Judges 3:15 (ESV)
Then the people of Israel cried out to the Lord, and the Lord raised up for them a deliverer, Ehud, the son of Gera, the Benjaminite, a left-handed man. The people of Israel sent tribute by him to Eglon the king of Moab.

The Lord raised up a man named Ehud, whose name means "united." He was from the tribe of Benjamin, one of the smaller tribes of the twelve and whose people seemed to carry a genetic link for left-handedness. Some say that the left-handedness of Benjaminites was due to their purposeful training. Scholars believe the ancient manuscripts which describe him as handicapped in his right hand, not ambidextrous.

Though we might not think of being left-handed as a handicap today, it has been listed in the past as a less desirable trait. In fact, elementary teachers in U.S. schools were trained in the 1900s to be on the lookout for left-handed pupils. If discovered, the teachers tried to influence them to use their right hand instead of their left hand for most applications.

Throughout history, left-handed people have been ridiculed and in the minority. Even so, there are many famous people who came to greatness who had the gene for left-handedness. People like:

President Garfield	President Hoover	President Reagan
President Truman	President Ford	President Bush Sr.
President Clinton	President Obama	Charlemagne
Alexander the Great	Napoleon Bonaparte	Queen Victoria
Prince Charles	Fidel Castro	Oprah Winfrey
Albert Schweitzer	Jay Leno	Mark Twain

Paul McCartney	Michelangelo	Tim Allen
Nicole Kidman	Larry Fine	Angelina Jolie
Bruce Willis	Scarlett Johansson	Morgan Freeman
Joan of Arc	Bill Gates	James Cameron
Jennifer Lawrence	Jimi Hendrix	Nikola Tesla

In ancient Palestine, to be left-handed was in some cases to be an outcast. However, God shows us in His Word that looking different or being different is not a reason to be ashamed. Jesus treated all people (apart from hypocrites) the same. So, Ehud did not let his "nonconformity" stand in his way of serving God.

Ehud also had a job as a tax collector for the king of Moab. In this position, he was again an outcast. Tax collectors have never been popular. Ehud would have been labeled a traitor to his own people because he collected money from the poor to give to King Eglon. No doubt those funds contributed to his overweight condition.

To understand how people felt about traitors, I suggest you watch the excellent WWII movie with William Holden, *Stalag 17*. The story is about a German concentration camp with many prisoners. One of the prisoners betrayed the captured allied soldiers. The film follows the mistaken idea that William Holden is the traitor. Because of their assumptions, he is mistreated and abused by his fellow men. *Stalag 17* demonstrates a society of people who cannot tolerate traitors.

In addition, tax collector Ehud would have been viewed as a traitor because it was a common practice for collectors to skim off the top profits for themselves. We don't know if Ehud actually did that.

Because of his employment, Ehud probably did not have many friends. Scripture tells us that he had servants to help him with the taxes, but these were likely professional acquaintances and not true friends. Tax collectors seemed to only have one or two other friends – other tax collectors.

Besides being left-handed, Ehud was also skilled in metal work. He made a special dagger for one purpose—to free Israel from oppression.

Judges 3:16 (ESV)
And Ehud made for himself a sword with two edges, a cubit in length, and he bound it on his right thigh under his clothes.

How long is a cubit? The Jewish cubit was about 18 inches in length. This was no pocketknife. It was a short, double-edged sword.

From the account, we know that God was a part of Ehud's life because he became one of the Judges of Israel. Guided by his purpose he felt was from God, this oddball set forth to free his country from King Eglon and the Moabites.

Judges 3:17-19 (ESV)
And he presented the tribute to Eglon king of Moab. Now Eglon was a very fat man. And when Ehud had finished presenting the tribute, he sent away the people who carried the tribute. But he himself turned back at the idols near Gilgal and said, "I have a secret message for you, O king." And he commanded, "Silence." And all his attendants went out from his presence.

On the last day of his employment to the Moabites, our hero was there as usual turning in the money he had collected from his district. Nothing was unusual or out of place. He departed with his assistants but left them after a short journey to return to King Eglon.

Notice he turned around at Gilgal, near the idols. Maybe seeing these detestable idols made him even angrier or, using a phrase I like, "righteously indignant." In any case, it was at the idols he put his righteous indignation into motion. He went back alone (he was probably used to that) to see Eglon again.

The ancient historian Josephus tells us that Ehud and Eglon were friends.

Now this man became familiar with Eglon, and that by means of presents, with which he obtained his favor, and insinuated himself into his good opinion; whereby he was also beloved of those that were about the king. [21]

Before Ehud informed Eglon of God's message, Eglon told everyone to leave them alone. Ehud must have known Eglon enough to anticipate this reaction, because they were now alone together.

Judges 3:20-22 (ESV)
And Ehud came to him as he was sitting alone in his cool roof chamber. And Ehud said, "I have a message from God for you." And he arose from his seat. And Ehud reached with his left hand, took the sword from his right thigh, and thrust it into his belly. And the hilt also went in after the blade, and the fat closed over the blade, for he did not pull the sword out of his belly; and the dung came out.

Now we see another trait of Ehud; he knew how to kill a man. He no doubt distracted Eglon with his right hand while with his left hand reached across his abdomen to remove the sword attached to his right thigh. Because Ehud's garment was concealing the sword, Eglon did not suspect anything. The king was fatally stabbed. Scripture is very descriptive here that Ehud left the sword in the belly of Eglon whose fat oozed out and closed over the blade. Graphic! God even tells us that his feces poured out of him. That is not an uncommon event when a person dies. It indicated that he was dead and not left alive to suffer. A blade eighteen inches long, thrust into a man's abdomen probably did irreparable damage to his arteries, veins, and nerves.

Judges 3:23-25 (ESV)
Then Ehud went out into the porch and closed the doors of the roof chamber behind him and locked them.

When he had gone, the servants came, and when they saw that the doors of the roof chamber were locked,

---

21 • Josephus, Flavius, and Whiston, William (1737). Anitquities of the Jews - Book V Ch 4 par 2. In *The Genuine Works of Flavius Josephus the Jewish Historian.*

they thought, "Surely he is relieving himself in the closet of the cool chamber." And they waited till they were embarrassed. But when he still did not open the doors of the roof chamber, they took the key and opened them, and there lay their lord dead on the floor.

Our hero made his escape and locked the doors behind him. Being that the feces of the man had poured out, the smell must have been quite strong. It was intense enough to make the servants of Eglon think he was going to the bathroom and wanted privacy. This gave Ehud the much-needed time to get away.

Judges 3:26-30 (ESV)
Ehud escaped while they delayed, and he passed beyond the idols and escaped to Seirah. When he arrived, he sounded the trumpet in the hill country of Ephraim. Then the people of Israel went down with him from the hill country, and he was their leader. And he said to them, "Follow after me, for the LORD has given your enemies the Moabites into your hand." So they went down after him and seized the fords of the Jordan against the Moabites and did not allow anyone to pass over. And they killed at that time about 10,000 of the Moabites, all strong, able-bodied men; not a man escaped. So Moab was subdued that day under the hand of Israel. And the land had rest for eighty years.

Ehud ran away, not to hide, but to form the militia for battle. Note that he did not go to his own tribe where he was probably an outcast. Instead, Ehud went to the tribe of Ephraim, a tribe with a great history of victories in battles. They immediately chose him to lead them into battle and soon afterwards the rest of Israel followed suit.

Our social outcast was the leader of the nation as he rallied the troops to follow him into battle and destroy the Moabite army.

There are seven distinct things we can say about this peculiar person. First, Ehud was from a tribe where the genetics of left-handedness was well known. The entire area is full of oddities. Second, the society of that time viewed his left-handedness as a handicap. Third, being a tax collector gave him the label as a despised traitor among his tribe. Fourth, he was probably a loner with few friends. Fifth, he excelled in metal shop classes as an elective. It was odd that Ehud crafted that knife as most Israelites had no idea how to forge metal. They often went to other countries to purchase metal items. Sixth, he was friendly with King Eglon, the enemy. What loyal citizen would not only collect taxes for the enemy but befriend the leader? Seventh, he knew how to kill a man. We're not told where he learned this, but he is very skilled at it. Eighth, he knew how to plan a righteous murder and make his escape. He preplanned all the events and fulfilled them perfectly. Ninth, despite being handicapped and despised among the Israelites, he had the charisma to organize an army of shepherds into a fighting machine. Tenth, he apparently had a close relationship with God, for God chose him to be the judge of Israel for the next several decades.

What kind of oddball are you? Do you think you are handicapped or unworthy in a way that prevents you from serving God or being His messenger? Have you been told by others that you don't fit in and thus are excluded by your peers? Have you convinced yourself that you just are not as talented as others to serve God in some key way?

I can think of two major types of people:

Oddball 1 • These people are afraid of being labeled as an outcast because of their relationship with God. Sometimes Christians feel that way. They feel their non-Christian friends won't accept them due to their relationship with Jesus, so they let their relationship with God dwindle and die off. Jesus knows that some people will not accept you as part of "the group" because of your relationship with Him, but Jesus said that anyone who would be ashamed of Him is not worthy of being His follower. Are you ashamed of the Gospel of Jesus Christ?

Oddball 2 • These are Christians that are not ashamed of the Gospel of Jesus Christ; it is the power of God unto salvation!

They refuse to be a secret Christian. They might dress different-ly than others. They may talk differently than others do. They might think differently than their peers. They refuse to compro-mise their beliefs for their friends. They read the Bible and may-be other books that their friends find objectionable. They can be found praying when others don't or when others make fun of them. They don't care what others say about them because they are going to live their lives for Jesus out in the open; they are going to stand and let the world know they are different!

O_2 is the symbol of atmospheric oxygen, a molecule necessary for fire and combustion. O_2 feeds a fire; remove it, and you extin-guish the fire. You, too, can be a necessary component to begin a fire for God. So, I challenge you to be an Oddball 2 or O_2 for God.

Arthur Blessitt not only led a future president to the Lord, but he also impacted many other people to serve Jesus. One young man heard him speak and was challenged to be an oddball for Christ in his high school. He was not ashamed of the Gospel of Jesus Christ, and he was not going to let his personal feelings stand in the way of his faith. He wore his Christianity on his sleeve be-cause his faith was so penetrating it went down to the bone. He witnessed and talked about Jesus in study halls. He shared Jesus with people at lunch. In speech class he preached sermons about Jesus and repentance. For book reports, he wrote on the book of Romans and James. He truly loved and cared for the people. He showed a loving Jesus to his schoolmates and his teachers. For this he was robbed, beaten, kicked, ridiculed, called names, spit upon, and ostracized. But when these things happened, he re-membered that people did the same things to Jesus, Paul, John, and others. He was a radically saved individual who would not back down about his faith or his commission in the Lord's Army. To this day, he is still teaching and preaching that same Gospel of Jesus Christ. Some say he is an oddball, and that does not bother him. There are a lot more like him around with even better sto-ries than his.

An old song I enjoy singing is *All Shook Up*. Not only is it the title of a song, but also a phrase in the song made popular by the late

Elvis Presley. Several years ago, an issue of Newsweek contained an interesting article about Elvis entitled, *All Shook-Up.*

Elvis Presley was born an only child and dirt-poor in a little town in Mississippi. At the young age of eighteen, while making fourteen dollars a week as a truck driver, he, just on a lark, decided to make a recording. That recording was all it took to vault him into becoming one of the best-paid male entertainers in the world. At age twenty-three he lost his mother.

Just before his death at age forty-two, he wished he could live one week of a normal life, walk up and down his city streets without being harassed. He said that he would pay a million dollars for just one week of peace.

Another entertainer named Pat Boone said of Elvis, "I cared a lot for Elvis." He said, "He went in the wrong direction. Ironically, we met for the last time when I was going to toward the East and he was on his way to Las Vegas. He said to me, 'Say, Pat, where are you going?' And I told him I was going to be involved in some kind of ministry. And he says to me, 'Hey, I am going to Las Vegas. Pat, as long as I've known you, you've been going in the wrong direction.' Pat Boone answered, 'Elvis, that just depends on where you're coming from and where you're going.'" [22]

Fan the Flame

Do you believe people think of you as an oddball? Why?

---

22 • *Newsweek*, August 29, 1977

Do you believe them?

_____

_____

_____

_____

_____

_____

How has it changed your behavior?

_____

_____

_____

_____

_____

_____

Despite his personal issues, Ehud didn't let them stop him from following God. Jot down some thoughts on how you can live your life for God despite your differences.

_____

_____

_____

_____

_____

_____

If you feel sad or depressed about the way others think or treat you, I encourage you to contact your pastor and set up a time to meet with him.

Naaman's Servant Girl
You Are the Right Age Now To Serve God

II Kings 5:1-5

There is a legend about Satan and his imps planning their strategy for attacking the world that's hearing the message of salvation. One of the demons says, "I've got the plan, Master. When I get on the earth and take charge of people's thinking, I'll tell them that there's no heaven."

The devil responds, "Ah, they'll never believe that. This Book of Truth is full of messages about the hope of heaven through sins forgiven. They won't believe that. They know there's a glory yet future."

On the other side of the room another says, "I've got the plan. I'll tell 'em there's no hell."

"No good," he says. "Jesus, while He was on earth, talked more of hell than of heaven. They know in their hearts that their wrongs will have to be taken care of in some way. They deserve nothing more than hell."

And one brilliant little imp in the back stood up and said, "Then I know the answer. I'll just tell them there's no hurry." And he's the one Satan chose.[23]

Over the chapters we have covered, we have seen many problems and excuses people may have that hinder their relationship with God. We have examined these lesser-known biblical characters while trying to find solutions to these problems and excuses. In this lesson we will zero in on a name that has been erased from history, but her story is one frequently taught to little children in Sunday Schools. The reason I chose the story of this little girl is that she is just that, a little girl who is not afraid nor ashamed to speak up about her faith. She was the little captive girl, stolen away from her land in Israel to serve as a slave to the commander-in-chief of the Syrian army. Even though times were bad for her, she kept her strong faith in her God. Let's read about this remarkable young girl.

II Kings 5:1-5 (ESV)

Naaman, commander of the army of the king of Syria, was a great man with his master and in high favor, because by him the Lord had given victory to Syria. He was a mighty man of valor, but he was a leper. Now the Syrians on one of their raids had carried off a little girl from the land of Israel, and she worked in the service of Naaman's wife. She said to her mistress, "Would that my lord were with the prophet who is in Samaria! He would cure him of his leprosy." So Naaman went in and told his lord, "Thus and so spoke the girl from the land of Israel." And the king of Syria said, "Go now, and I will send a letter to the king of Israel." So he went, taking with him ten talents of silver, six thousand shekels of gold, and ten changes of clothes.

I can't help but be amazed at this young child. First, we don't know her name, but we can get an idea of her age. The Hebrew word used to describe her is הַנַּעֲרָ **Na'arah**, pronounced 'nah-ar-aw' and usually is used to indicate a girl aged from infancy to

---

23 • Lewis, C. S. (1995). *The screwtape Letters.* Bantam Books.

adolescence. Thus, we have a young adolescent girl who had a great deal of knowledge about the prophet Elisha in her own country. Another amazing feature that is often overlooked is that she most likely never saw or even heard of Elisha healing a person with leprosy.

This young girl had remarkable faith in God. I can't help but wonder what kind of witness this young girl was to this gentile family in the city of Damascus, the capital of Aram. Her owner and probable capturer, Naaman, must have thought this girl was different from the start. He took her from her family in Israel and gave her to his wife as a gift. It is possible that he even was responsible for the death of this girl's parents. What did they talk about, this mistress of the house and this young adolescent girl? What conversations did they hold? What was her role? We are not told. We can assume that she must have been a good servant for Naaman, the commander-in-chief of the army, to listen to her. He must have had some respect for her to take her seriously. And Naaman possibly even took her to see the king about her faith! What a witness! Unfortunately, you don't see faith like that too often. So, what can we gather about this young girl?

There are ten things that stand out to me about this young girl that I want to make note of.

First, the Syrian army under Naaman was responsible for kidnapping her and possibly killing her family. Syria was the enemy of Israel and a foreign land where idols were worshipped.

Second, she was a young girl, preadolescent and was not of age to be married yet.

Third, though she was young, she had a remarkably strong faith in God, even in the foreign land. Surrounded by idols, unusual customs, and a foreign culture, her faith in God had not swayed.

Fourth, she had a very good knowledge of the power of the true God and His prophet Elisha. Where did she get this? Certainly, she was taught these things from an early age by her parents and family. We can see how important it is for parents to root our children in the knowledge of God and His Word. As it is written...

Proverbs 22:6 (ESV)
Train up a child in the way he should go; even
when he is old he will not depart from it.

Kudos to this young girl's parents and/or family upbringing. I hope all Christian parents take that verse to heart in this lesson. It is true that even with a strong Christian upbringing, some teens and young adults walk away from the Lord. I have witnessed this too often. Much of the time it was due to the students relying on the faith of their parents instead of making their faith solidly their own. There is not a failsafe against Satan's attack to turn young minds, but helping children learn the truth of God and His Word and teaching them good apologetics can add to the Armor of God that they should be wearing daily.

Fifth, did you notice that this young preadolescent was not hostile to her capturer? She seemed to have accepted her new surroundings and new home, but she was still loyal to her God. She appeared to hold no grudge against this man who killed her people. She knew the power of God to do the impossible, but she seemed to accept her path and situation as God's will. How many times do unbelievers and even Christians today blame God for not preventing a disaster in their lives, or worse, believe He was powerless to help? We can see here that God has a plan. As Paul writes in Romans...

Romans 8:28 (GW)
We know that all things work together for
the good of those who love God—those whom
he has called according to his plan.

God's plan is a mystery to us because we cannot see the whole picture with our finite eyes and lives. But He is in control, and He can use what we call disasters to glorify Himself, which is our purpose in life. As the old hymns state, "We will understand it better by and by." Or "Farther along we'll understand why."

Sixth, she was full of compassion for her new master. How can this be? She treated the man responsible for killing her people and family with kindheartedness. This is amazing! Yet, it is the same message Jesus tells us to do when He said to "love your enemies, do good to those who hate you" (Luke 6:27).

Seventh, she was not afraid to stand up and proclaim her faith even when in the minority. She was living in a heathen land where God was not worshipped. Still, she vocalized her faith to the commander-in-chief of the enemy. He could have punished her for doing so in many ways, but he did not. He listened then acted on her witness. Oh, that we Christians would not be apprehensive in sharing our faith even when we are outnumbered by the adversary.

Eighth, did you see that this young preadolescent was expecting God to heal Naaman? Had she ever seen Elisha before? Had she ever witnessed God healing a person through Elisha? Not that we are told. But that was where her faith was. She did not wait for a vision or sign from God to tell her to make this claim. She took a step of faith based upon what she had been taught and heard back home when she was young and free. I am so impressed with this girl's humble faith in God. Though she was young and a small child, she was a giant in faith.

Ninth, have you noticed the respect she gave to her enemies? Most would wish leprosy upon all the people of Syria, but she was trying to help the commander-in-chief be rid of his disease. Even as a slave her beliefs were greatly different from her capturers. She showed them honor, compassion and respect.

Lastly, tenth, she appeared to be a good servant. Why would Naaman listen to a slave girl who was a miserable, goldbricking, meritless rat? He would not. She appeared to be honorable in her work, which led this esteemed and respected general to not only listen to her but to heed her words and act upon them.

How can you not be impressed with this little girl? And because of her faith in God, she was responsible for the salvation of

Naaman, the commander-in-chief of the Syrian army. Little did he dream that when he took this little girl home, she would be the instrument by which God would claim his soul. As a result of this unnamed girl, we will likely see Naaman in heaven one day. All by the faith of someone who didn't think she was too young to serve the Lord at her age.

God gives us other examples of how people of all ages, especially young ones, can be used for His service. Just a few are:

- Samuel was dedicated just as he was weaned from Hannah his mother.
- Jeremiah was a young boy when God called him to be his speaker.
- A little unnamed boy gave Jesus his lunch to feed 5,000 and was instrumental in a great miracle.
- Paul was saved when his young nephew informs others of the enemy's plot to murder him.
- Moses was saved at birth, but he did not enter ministry until he was 80.
- David was a lad when anointed king of Israel.
- Jesus Himself shocked the elders at the Temple at His young age with His knowledge.

Yet too often I hear people say, "I am too young or too old to be used by God." Others might say, "I'll serve God later. I want to live my life first." That last one is one of the most selfish statements I have ever heard. Two of the seven words of that short statement are personal pronouns. That is spoken like a true, self-centered, selfish individual who is an infant in their walk.

The real tragedy is that we are finite beings who do not know how long we will be allowed to work on this earth. As a teacher in schools for 25 years, I have been saddened many times when a student died prematurely. While in high school, I witnessed many students who died from natural and unnatural causes. Sophomore Diana Biggerstaff died of a congenital heart disease no one knew she had. Junior Bridgett Regli was murdered because she photographed a drug transaction on school grounds. One friend died from the flu. Other friends died at their own hands by committing suicide. Still more were killed in car accidents. The truth is that we don't know how long we have on this planet or what God's plan is for us.

There is an old saying, "Only one life will soon be past. Only what's done for Christ will last." That statement has a ring of truth in it. How committed are you to Jesus Christ? The little, young slave girl didn't leave her commitment to God back in Israel; she took it with her even to the evil city of Damascus. She refused to back down in her faith, regardless of what the other slaves or even the family she worked for thought. She was committed to God at all costs! How committed are you?

It's tough to live a focused life. From every direction something or someone clamors for our attention. A distraction draws our eyes and the next thing we know, we've swerved off the road and headed down another detour.

A long time ago I heard Chuck Swindoll tell a special story that is interesting and has a good point.

> *One Chicago youth pastor came up with a clever way to keep his group on track. Concerned that the balmy beaches of Florida – the site of their upcoming evangelism trip – would lure the teens from their purpose, he fashioned a cross from two pieces of lumber. Just before they got on the bus, he showed it to the group.*
>
> *"I want all of you to remember that the whole purpose of our going is to glorify the name of Christ, to lift up the cross – the message of the Cross, the emphasis of the Cross, the Christ of the Cross," he announced. "So, we're going to take this cross wherever we go."*
>
> *The teenagers looked at one another, a little unsure of his plan. But they agreed to do it and dragged the cross on the bus. It banged back and forth in the aisle all the*

way to Florida. It went with them into restaurants. It stayed overnight where they stayed overnight. It stood in the sand while they ministered on the beach.

At first, lugging the cross around embarrassed the kids. But later, it became a point of identification. That cross was a constant, silent reminder of who they were and why they had come. They eventually regarded carrying it as an honor and privilege.

The night before they went home, the youth leader handed out two nails to each of the kids. He told them that if they wanted to commit themselves to what the cross stood for, they could hammer one nail into it and keep the other with them. One by one, the teens drove their nails into the cross.

About fifteen years later, one fellow – now a stockbroker – called the youth leader. He told him that he still keeps that nail with him in his desk drawer. Whenever he loses his sense of focus, he looks at the nail and remembers the cross on that beach in Florida. It reminds him of what is at the core of his life – his commitment to Jesus Christ.[24]

Not too long ago, I spoke about serving God to a church full of young adults. After the service a man came up to me and greeted me with a handshake. He told me that years ago he served one summer at the Christian camp in the northwoods of Wisconsin where I worked. He related how that summer he dedicated his life to serving Jesus after hearing me speak. He told me that I had set up a crude cross and had passed out two nails to everyone. He said that I laid down a hammer and told the group that if they wanted to commit their lives to Christ, to come and hammer one nail into the cross as a symbol of their commitment, but to keep the other nail with them to remind them of this decision.

---

24 • Swindoll, C. R. (1998). Authenticity. In *Swindoll's Ultimate book of illustrations & quotes: Over 1,500 outstanding ways to effectively drive home your message* (pp. 97). T. Nelson.

Almost two decades came and went and, honestly, I could not recall him, but I did tell him I could recall the night I did this at a Bible study with the camp staff. Then he reached into a pocket and pulled out his wallet. From the wallet, he retrieved an old nail. He told me that this was the companion nail to the one he hammered into the cross that night. He expressed to me that he carries this nail with him everywhere he goes and how it reminds him of the decision he made that night. He said that when he is tempted or becomes weak, he pulls out that nail and it reminds him of what Christ did for him on the cross and that he will always live for Him.

Fan the Flame

Have you ever spoken about your faith or the faith of another follower of God to someone else? Describe the circumstance.

Are you aware of anything you've said or done that keeps people from listening or respecting you? Jot down the incident(s). Be specific. If possible, share your results with a respected Christian for their feedback.

How can you stay firm in your faith despite your circumstances? Paul stated some wonderful ways in Ephesians 6:10-18. Make a list and consider how each one can help you.

Do you need a reminder of your faith like the nail the man carried in his wallet? Find something meaningful to you and keep it in sight. It could be an object, Bible verse, or phrase.

Mary

As a small boy, one of the highlights of my life was riding with my parents to visit my granny six hours away in southern Illinois. She was widowed before I was born and lived in a large house heated by coal fireplaces. She was quite old and could not see well, but I can still remember her sitting in her rocking chair near the fireplace or, in the summer, on a porch swing.

One time when I was quite small, I settled down in front of her rocking chair where she sat with her Bible and magnifying glass. As she looked at me with faded eyes, I said, "Do you remember being a little girl about my age?" She nodded that she did. (For someone very old, she had a mind that was as sharp as a tack.) I asked her to tell me what she remembered when she was a little girl. As she leaned back in her large chair, she glanced around the room. I could tell memories were flooding her mind. Then she began telling me about a parade that she went to during the Spanish-American War. She spoke of when soldiers paraded through the streets of her small town on their way to fight. She talked about what she used to do as chores around her house growing up, like churning butter and feeding animals. She told stories of berry picking and playing with other children. She went on and on for a long time. I was fascinated as I took in story after story. Some of my favorite stories were about her relationship and dependency upon God. She really wanted to instill that in me. She succeeded. I have one of her Bibles that she read and the magnifying glass she used to read it. The impact from those moments is still being played out today as you listen to me speak or read what I write in this ministry. Sitting at the feet of my Granny Lane was a happy, precious, and soothing place. I can almost feel the warmth and see the glow of the fire.

The New Testament contains many women named Mary. The character we will study was the sister of Martha who shared their home with their brother Lazarus in Bethany. This Mary is mentioned on three occasions, and on each occasion, we see her at the feet of Jesus. She is always positively portrayed, and we have much to learn about our relationship with Jesus by examining her life.

We are first introduced to Mary when Jesus and His entourage visited the village of Bethany, just about two miles east of Jerusalem and on the opposite side of the Mount of Olives. Luke records this famous event.

Luke 10: 38-42 (ESV)
Now as they went on their way, Jesus entered a village. And a woman named Martha welcomed him into her house. And she had a sister called Mary, who sat at the Lord's feet and listened to his teaching. But Martha was distracted with much serving. And she went up to him and said, "Lord, do you not care that my sister has left me to serve alone? Tell her then to help me." But the Lord answered her, "Martha, Martha, you are anxious and troubled about many things, but one thing is necessary. Mary has chosen the good portion, which will not be taken away from her."

Martha appears to be the head of the house as she was mentioned first, and the house is called hers. In John's gospel, we read that they had a brother named Lazarus as well, who also appeared to be younger than Martha.

As the passage in Luke unfolds, Martha was preparing a meal for Jesus and His followers. In Bible times, guests were welcomed into homes with food and beverages. It appears that Martha was going a little overboard in her preparation. Mary, who would have normally been helping Martha in this preparation, had removed herself from this duty and was found sitting at Jesus' feet and listening to Him teach. This infuriated Martha and she asked Jesus to reprimand Mary. Instead, He supported Mary's decision. Let us examine what it meant for Mary to sit at the feet of Jesus.

To sit at a Rabbi's feet in the first century A.D. meant you were a disciple of that Rabbi. Notice when Jesus healed the demon possessed man in Gerasenes, the people found him sitting quietly at the feet of Jesus.

Luke 8:35 (ESV)
Then people went out to see what had happened, and they came to Jesus and found the man from whom the demons had gone, sitting at the feet of Jesus, clothed and in his right mind, and they were afraid.

Likewise, Paul, when speaking of his training as a Pharisee, described himself sitting at the feet of his teacher.

Acts 22:3 (ESV)
"I am a Jew, born in Tarsus in Cilicia, but brought up in this city, educated at the feet of Gamaliel according to the strict manner of the law of our fathers, being zealous for God as all of you are this day."

The amazing thing is that women during this time were not usually permitted to be disciples of a rabbi. Jesus broke down the barrier of this man-made law by allowing women to sit and learn at His feet. In fact, He welcomed it and praised Mary for doing it.

Women in the Jewish culture at the time of Christ were often not looked upon with favor. In his book, *Jerusalem in the Time of Jesus*, Dr. Jeremias states, "The woman's position in the house corresponded to exclusion...of public life...Their education was limited to domestic arts, especially needlework, and weaving... food and drink." There is more. In the ancient Jewish Mishnah, Sotah 3:4 states that "if any man gives his daughter a knowledge of the Law it is as though he taught her lechery." This, of course, is not God's plan but was man's additional laws put upon that society. Thus, with this stereotype, Mary sitting and learning at the feet of Jesus went against the culture of the day. In fact, Jesus shattered the cultural standard of women and encouraged women to assume a disciple's position. Later in that century and into the beginning of the next, many of the leadership roles in churches throughout the Roman Empire were held by women.

Some examples of women leaders are found in the New Testament:

1. Anna was a prophetess who served God at the Temple and declared Jesus as the Son of God (Luke 2:36-38).

2. The four daughters of Philip the evangelist who prophesied for God (Acts 21:8-9).

3. The women at the garden tomb instructed and told the disciples that Jesus was indeed alive. Jesus instructed them to give His disciples a message (John 20:17-18).

4. Apphia in Philemon 2 was a leader of the church in Colossae.

5. Nympha allowed and hosted a church to meet in her house in Laodicea (Colossians 4:15).

6. Priscilla, the wife of Aquila, helped teach the great evangelist Apollos about Jesus (Acts 18:26). She had a church meeting in her house (I Corinthians 16:19). Paul even called her a "fellow worker" in advancing the gospel (Romans 16:3).

7. Phoebe was a key leader in the church at Cenchreae (Romans 16:1-2). Paul actually called her by the male title of *diakonos*. This is the Greek word from where we get the church office called Deacon. (The word deacon did not come into existence until the later part of the 4th century A.D.) She was also referred to as a *prostatis*, which is a person in authority over others, in this case she is in authority over some members of the church. In early church history, records show that it was she to whom Paul chose to deliver the Epistle to the Romans for him from Corinth to Rome. Even Origen, who was hardly "pro-woman," saw Phoebe as

having apostolic authority (*Commentarium in Epistolam B. Pauli ad Romanos* 10:1278).

8. Lydia of Philippi taught and converted her entire household to Christ in Acts 16.

9. Euodia and Syntyche "contended at my side in the cause of the gospel, along with Clement and the rest of my fellow workers" (Philippians 4:2-3). Paul equates their roles with Priscilla.

10. Junia, another helper of Paul in his ministry, was named as a form of an "apostle." The Greek word used here is **ἀπόστολος apostolos** though she appears to be a minor one (Romans 16:7).

11. The woman at the well in John 4, who went forth to witness, teach, and explain to her townsfolk that the Messiah has come!

Indeed, Jesus broke the tradition of what was taught in the traditional Jewish Law.

Now back to our study. Notice what Mary was doing in Luke 10; she was listening to God speak. Martha could have and should have done the same, but she was too wrapped up in setting the table, preparing the meal, etc. She missed the important thing – listening to God. And when Martha tried to get Jesus to reprimand Mary, Jesus reprimanded Martha instead. He said:

Luke 10:42 (GWT)
There's only one thing you need [worth worrying about]. Mary has made the right choice, and that one thing will not be taken away from her."

There is a faith lesson here for us. Too often we get caught up in things that are not important instead of dealing with the single most important thing – listening to God. However, before we judge Martha and demean her, we need to examine ourselves. What gets in my way of listening to God? What stops or hinders me from reading and studying His Word? What takes priority over my relationship with God? God is telling us that sitting at the feet of Jesus and taking in His words are more important than other things. How our lives would change if we just set our priorities in order to God's design.

The next time we read about Mary is in John 11 and deals with the raising of her brother Lazarus from the dead.

John 11:1-32 (ESV)

Now a certain man was ill, Lazarus of Bethany, the village of Mary and her sister Martha. It was Mary who anointed the Lord with ointment and wiped his feet with her hair, whose brother Lazarus was ill. So the sisters sent to him, saying, "Lord, he whom you love is ill." But when Jesus heard it he said, "This illness does not lead to death. It is for the glory of God, so that the Son of God may be glorified through it."

Now Jesus loved Martha and her sister and Lazarus. So, when he heard that Lazarus was ill, he stayed two days longer in the place where he was...

[17] Now when Jesus came, he found that Lazarus had already been in the tomb four days. Bethany was near Jerusalem, about two miles off, and many of the Jews had come to Martha and Mary to console them concerning their brother. So when Martha heard that Jesus was coming, she went and met him, but Mary remained seated in the house. Martha said to Jesus, "Lord, if you had been here, my brother would not have died. But even now I know that whatever you ask from God, God will give you." Jesus said to her, "Your brother will rise again." Martha said to him, "I know that he will rise again in the resurrection on the last day." Jesus said to her, "I am the resurrection and the life. Whoever believes in me, though he die, yet shall he live, and everyone who lives and believes in me shall never die. Do you believe this?" She said to him, "Yes, Lord; I believe that you are the Christ, the Son of God, who is coming into the world."

When she had said this, she went and called her sister Mary, saying in private, "The Teacher is here and is calling for you."

And when she heard it, she rose quickly and went to him. Now Jesus had not yet come into the village, but was still in the place where Martha had met him. When the Jews who were with her in the house, consoling her, saw Mary rise quickly and go out, they followed her, supposing that she was going to the tomb to weep there. Now when Mary came to where Jesus was and saw him, she fell at his feet, saying to him, "Lord, if you had been here, my brother would not have died."

In this passage we read that Lazarus has died. Martha and Mary had sent word to Jesus for Him to come and heal their brother, but Jesus delayed His coming to make sure that Lazarus was dead. There was no doubt he was dead because he had been in a tomb for four days. Also, the reason Jesus waited until Lazarus was dead four days was to deal with the Jewish myth that the soul hung around the body for three days, hoping to find a way back into it. Thus, by day four, all hope of resuscitating was gone, and the body was already being broken down by bacterial and enzymatic action.

We find Martha meeting Jesus on the road after leaving the duties of mourning. She had learned from her last encounter with Jesus that it was best to meet and talk with Him.

After speaking with Jesus, she returned to the house where Mary was sitting with many mourners. Martha whispered into her ear that Jesus had come and wanted to see her. Mary quickly rose to meet her Lord and fell at His feet. She echoed Martha's complaint about Jesus being too slow or waiting too long to help. No doubt Martha had influenced her little sister. Grief causes people to react in different ways. The point is that we again find Mary at the feet of Jesus. Jesus had a plan for the Jewish leaders as well as the scores of people watching that would bring Him glory. Lazarus was raised from the dead! Had Jesus come on the time schedule that Mary and Martha designed and wanted, this miracle would not have taken place. Look what happened as a result of God's planning this event.

John 11: 45 (ESV)
Many of the Jews therefore, who had come with
Mary and had seen what he did, believed in him.

As we have seen, God sometimes places difficulties in our lives to bring Him glory. These times are not pleasant as we go through them, and we often don't understand when He is silent or seemingly deaf to our prayers. In such times, we need to realize that He is in control, and He has a plan that works for good. It may not be the good we wish, but it is the good that glorifies Him and adds to His kingdom. We simply must learn what the old hymn says, to trust and obey.

The third time we come across Mary is shortly after the raising of Lazarus. John records this amazing event.

John 12: 1-8 (ESV)
Six days before the Passover, Jesus therefore came to Bethany, where Lazarus was, whom Jesus had raised from the dead. So they gave a dinner for him there. Martha served, and Lazarus was one of those reclining with him at table. Mary therefore took a pound of expensive ointment made from pure nard, and anointed the feet of Jesus and wiped his feet with her hair. The house was filled with the fragrance of the perfume. But Judas Iscariot, one of his disciples (he who was about to betray him), said, "Why was this ointment not sold for three hundred denarii and given to the poor?" He said this, not because he cared about the poor, but because he was a thief, and having charge of the moneybag he used to help himself to what was put into it. Jesus said, "Leave her alone, so that she may keep it for the day of my burial. For the poor you always have with you, but you do not always have me."

Many of us know this story, but most do not understand what Mary was actually doing. This event happened shortly before Jesus went to the cross. During the meal, which we again see Martha serving, Mary took about 12oz of perfume or nard, worth about a year's wages today, and poured it on Jesus's feet. This is the equivalent today of taking a 12oz bottle of Chanel Grand Extrait perfume, which costs $4,200/oz, and pouring it on Jesus's feet. The Gospel of Mark includes that she also anointed His head, but John is focusing on what she does here with His feet.

Anointing Jesus's feet was a custom of the day but not with such a costly gift. Usually, it was simply done with water or olive oil. John is telling us a couple of important things here. First, Mary anointed Jesus with what must have been her most precious gift. What did she do with the costly and precious item? She surrendered it and offered it all to Jesus. In Mark 14:3, we are told that she actually broke the vessel, a selfless sacrifice to God. This was a form of worship. The disciples didn't sit around the table singing choruses, but it was done in awe and probably silence. We know that some like Judas were shocked by this.

Again, here is an important lesson for us to grasp and implement in our lives. Mary sacrificed her treasure in an act of worship. What do you have that you refuse to part with? Or have you offered everything on the altar to Him?

Second, notice how Mary wipes the feet of Jesus. It was customary to wash an honored guest's feet and dry them with a towel. I am fairly certain Mary had towels in the house, but she willingly chose something different and for a good reason. It says, "wiped his feet with her hair." Have you ever thought about that? Why her hair? What significance or meaning could that possibly make?

To understand this, you need to go back and examine ancient Jewish culture. To ancient Jews, a woman's hair was her glory. We also see this in Scripture.

I Corinthians 11:15 (NKJV)
But if a woman has long hair, it is a glory to her;
for her hair is given to her for a covering.

Jewish women would seldom cut their hair because it was their glory. Now, what is Mary doing? She has already poured out her treasure to Jesus, then she knelt at the feet of Jesus and relinquished her glory to Him. This was one of the most descriptive and beautiful examples of worship recorded in Scripture. Kneeling at the feet of Jesus. Offering Him our most precious possession. Surrendering to Him our glory.

Let's learn from Mary's example here. Have you knelt and humbled yourself to Jesus? Have you offered up all on the altar to Him? Have you surrendered your glory to Him? Have you committed your life and trusted in Him as your Savior? If not, what is keeping you from doing so?

Mary is a lesser character mentioned only a few times in Scripture, but many can recall her name. She taught us that we need to often sit at the feet of Jesus, listen and commune with Him. She taught us that even though we walk with God, we will go through sad and tough times in which God seems to be silent, waiting for us to trust and obey him. She also taught a valuable lesson in worship and sacrificing our all to Jesus.

There is a hymn that appears to have been written in 1868 by a man named J.L. Hall. Though he wrote many hymns during his life, this one has some mystery. Unlike some other famous hymns that have stories behind them, *Sitting at the Feet of Jesus* has no surviving account. All we have here is just the simple, sweet lyrics of a meditation. I can think of no better way to end this lesson.

Sitting at the feet of Jesus,
Oh, what words I hear Him say!
Happy place! so near, so precious!
May it find me there each day;
Sitting at the feet of Jesus,
I would look upon the past;
For His love has been so gracious,
It has won my heart at last.

Sitting at the feet of Jesus,
Where can mortal be more blest?
There I lay my sins and sorrows,
And, when weary, find sweet rest;

Sitting at the feet of Jesus,
There I love to weep and pray;
While I from His fullness gather
Grace and comfort every day.

Bless me, O my Savior, bless me,
As I sit low at Thy feet;
Oh, look down in love upon me,
Let me see Thy face so sweet;
Give me, Lord, the mind of Jesus,
Keep me holy as He is;
May I prove I've been with Jesus,
Who is all my righteousness.

Fan the Flame

What things in your life keep you from spending time with Jesus?

_____

_____

_____

_____

_____

_____

Have you had a tragedy or very difficult experience in your life? Read John 11:28-36. How did Mary deal with her loss? What was Jesus's response?

_____

_____

_____

_____

_____

Have you ever given a sacrificial gift to someone? Why did you do it? What did it cost you?

Read Romans 12:1 What does Paul say we should do as an act of worship?

Martha

Years ago, when I taught biological sciences, I often allowed certain students to help me prepare chemicals and equipment, create media for cultures, and clean the lab. I primarily taught my lessons through a "hands-on" approach instead of a straight lecture. This teaching technique required time-consuming lab preparations.

One year I chose a girl to help me whom we'll call Connie. Connie and I got along very well. She was sweet and smart, which I hoped would be a good fit for my purpose. However, I soon began to notice something about her. Although she cleaned and mixed the chemicals, some labs failed because she did not follow my directions exactly. Her work was excellent, but she wanted to accomplish her own agenda instead of following directions. She didn't listen. I know she was trying to impress me, but instead of easing my workload, her lack of obedience made my life quite stressful. I ended up having to dismiss her, all because she wouldn't listen to me.

Martha was a popular character in the Gospels, but most people know very little about her life. We first meet Martha in Luke's gospel in a telling story that defines her and another woman.

Luke 10: 38-42 (ESV)
*Now as they went on their way, Jesus entered a village.
And a woman named Martha welcomed him into her house.
And she had a sister called Mary, who sat at the Lord's feet
and listened to his teaching. But Martha was distracted*

with much serving. And she went up to him and said, "Lord, do you not care that my sister has left me to serve alone? Tell her then to help me." But the Lord answered her, "Martha, Martha, you are anxious and troubled about many things, but one thing is necessary. Mary has chosen the good portion, which will not be taken away from her."

The first thing we notice in this passage is that there is a village. This village is later identified as Bethany, which is located just a couple of miles from Jerusalem on the eastern side of the Mount of Olives.

Next, we read that Martha is mentioned first and that she welcomed Jesus (which would have included His entourage) into her house. Notice that it states that it was **her house**. She apparently was the head mistress of the home. There was no mention of a husband, who, if she was married, would have certainly been identified as the head of the house. Most women in those days were married in their early teens, some as early as twelve years old. Some preach that women did not own homes, but this is not correct. In fact, the New Testament lists several women in high social standing such as Mary Magdalene, Chloe, Nympha, and Lydia who owned homes. We also know from the gospel writers that Jesus had some women who supported Him and His ministry.

Luke 8: 1-3 (ESV)
Soon afterward he went on through cities and villages, proclaiming and bringing the good news of the kingdom of God. And the twelve were with him, and also some women who had been healed of evil spirits and infirmities: Mary, called Magdalene, from whom seven demons had gone out, and Joanna, the wife of Chuza, Herod's household manager, and Susanna, and many others, who provided for them out of their means.

What was Martha doing when she invited Jesus into her house? She was not only inviting Jesus into her home, but also serving a meal to the entire group. Even today in Israel, it is a common custom to offer drinks and food to guests. Her concern was to serve Jesus. Often Martha is singled out in the story as doing something wrong. She was not doing anything wrong; she was fulfilling the custom by serving Jesus.

In verse thirty-nine we read that Martha had a sister named Mary. By the style of this writing, we can guess that Mary was younger than Martha. But look where Luke places Mary. She was sitting at the feet of Jesus. Again, too often we hold Mary in higher regard than Martha because she was sitting at the feet of Jesus. Really, who could fault her for doing this? Jesus even commended and blessed her for this. Then we get on Martha's case again.

What do you think Mary had been doing before sitting at Jesus's feet? She was most likely helping in the kitchen because Jesus would have had His disciples with Him. We are not just making a case of placing another plate at the table or "putting another tater in the pot" as my mom used to say. It is likely that Martha was motivated to prepare a more elaborate meal than was necessary. Why do people do such things? We are not told for sure here, but most likely people do it to impress someone. I remember when my wife and I were dating. One night early in our relationship, I tried to impress her with an extraordinary dinner. It really did not make her like me more. Similarly, Martha could have just made the meal simple and then joined Mary at Jesus' feet, but she didn't.

Apparently, while working in the kitchen, Mary seemed to have wandered off and Martha saw her sitting at the feet of Jesus. This caused Martha to fume as she did all the work and served as well. So, she asked Jesus for help. Martha seemed to be upset that both Mary and Jesus are resetting the cultural boundaries of the day.

Notice that Martha was being hospitable and serving Jesus. These are two great gifts. In this culture, this was actually the sacred duty of the woman of the house. She was performing a commendable task. We should not condemn her for this, but she did have her priorities a little mixed up. Notice how she handled the situation.

Luke 10:40b (ESV)
And she went up to him and said, "Lord, do you not care that
my sister has left me to serve alone? Tell her then to help me."

Did you notice that she corrected Jesus and told her Lord what to do? I am sure none of us are guilty of such behavior (sarcasm intended). Martha was not afraid to tell Him she believed He was making a mistake. John's gospel also records the story of Jesus raising her brother Lazarus from the dead. He had been dead for four days when Jesus arrived at her house. Lazarus was already buried and in the tomb. Look at how she addressed Jesus.

John 11:21 (ESV)
Martha said to Jesus, "Lord, if you had been
here, my brother would not have died.

She seems to be telling Him that He should have planned his travel schedule better so that Lazarus would not have died. However, she was not done correcting Jesus. When Jesus said roll the stone away, look at her response.

John 11:39 (ESV)
Jesus said, "Take away the stone." Martha, the sister
of the dead man, said to him, "Lord, by this time there
will be an odor, for he has been dead four days."

Martha tried to correct Jesus by telling Him that the body would have a stench by that time.

Do you understand what Martha is doing? She had no problem correcting God. This seemed to be an area of trouble for Martha in her spiritual life. She wanted to serve the Lord, which is commendable and correct; but when Jesus directed her to do something that didn't seem right to her, she responded by telling God where He was making a mistake.

Now, before we jump all over poor Martha, I do want to point out three admirable characteristics I see in her. First, the second time Jesus and His entourage come to Bethany and stay at her house, Martha seems to have learned from her mistake about serving dinner.

John 12:1-3 (GW)

Six days before Passover, Jesus arrived in Bethany. Lazarus, whom Jesus had brought back to life, lived there. Dinner was prepared for Jesus in Bethany. Martha served the dinner, and Lazarus was one of the people eating with Jesus. Mary took a bottle of very expensive perfume made from pure nard and poured it on Jesus' feet. Then she dried his feet with her hair. The fragrance of the perfume filled the house.

The house full of people being served dinner, and Mary appeared to be sitting at the feet of Jesus again. Martha though did not get upset this time. She had apparently learned her lesson. Serving was her act of worship, a spiritual gift God places in some people (Romans 12:7). It is interesting that the Greek word used is **διακονία**, pronounced *dee-ak-on-ee'-ah*, and literally means to "wait on tables."

The second admirable thing I want to point out concerning Martha is her faith. In John 11, we read the sad story of the death of Lazarus.

John 11:1-27 (ESV)

Now a certain man was ill, Lazarus of Bethany, the village of Mary and her sister Martha. It was Mary who anointed the Lord with ointment and wiped his feet with her hair, whose brother Lazarus was ill. So the sisters sent to him, saying, "Lord, he whom you love is ill." But when Jesus heard it he said, "This illness does not lead to death. It is for the glory of God, so that the Son of God may be glorified through it."

Now Jesus loved Martha and her sister and Lazarus. So, when he heard that Lazarus was ill, he stayed two days longer in the place where he was... [17] Now when Jesus came, he found that Lazarus had already been in the tomb four days. Bethany was near Jerusalem, about two miles off, and many of the Jews had come to Martha and Mary

*to console them concerning their brother. So when Martha
heard that Jesus was coming, she went and met him, but
Mary remained seated in the house. Martha said to Jesus,
"Lord, if you had been here, my brother would not have
died. But even now I know that whatever you ask from
God, God will give you." Jesus said to her, "Your brother
will rise again." Martha said to him, "I know that he will
rise again in the resurrection on the last day." Jesus said to
her, "I am the resurrection and the life. Whoever believes
in me, though he die, yet shall he live, and everyone who
lives and believes in me shall never die. Do you believe
this?" She said to him, "Yes, Lord; I believe that you are the
Christ, the Son of God, who is coming into the world."*

Notice who met Jesus along the road to Bethany. It was Martha.
Mary stayed in the house and did not come to meet Him. Martha's old habits began to appear when she tried to correct Jesus.
After this, look at the faith Martha expressed to Jesus: "I believe
that you are the Christ, the Son of God, who is coming into the
world." This is an amazing statement. It is so similar to what Peter responded to Jesus at Caesarea Philippi.

Matthew 16:15-16 (ESV)
*He said to them, "But who do you say that I am?"
Simon Peter replied, "You are the Christ,
the Son of the living God."*

The third element I want to mention is how Martha had grown.
Look carefully at her response when Jesus drew near after her
brother's death.

John 11:20 (ESV)
*So when Martha heard that Jesus was coming, she went
and met him, but Mary remained seated in the house.*

In those days it was the custom of the deceased family to sit on
the floor or a low chair in their house when mourning the loss
of a loved one. Friends would come over and grieve with them.
(This is still a custom among some in the Middle East and Juda-

ism today. It is called *shivah* and it is very therapeutic for the releasing of grief.) Mary stayed in the house following the cultural custom, while Martha rose and went to Jesus.

What can we learn from Martha? I will cite three major lessons we can learn from her. First, Martha was teachable. When God taught her something, she not only learned it, but she later put it into action. Too often people will read the Word of God, hear God tell them of some change in their life they need to make, but refuse to ever change. They are not teachable.

Second, Martha wanted to serve God. This is commendable, but it must be balanced with sitting at the feet of Jesus. Communing with Jesus, reading His Word and praying are so important. Too often Christians, pastors, and missionaries get too caught up in serving that they neglect their relationship with Jesus. We must never do that; there is a balance.

Third, often people will look at Martha as a worker and Mary as a worshipper. They then assume that we should be one or the other. I disagree. I believe we should be both at the same time. Serving is a form of worship, but Martha needed to learn to balance that with listening and implementing what Jesus told her.

Connie had the same problem that Martha had. Though she served well, she couldn't balance her willingness to serve with listening to what I required her to do.

During the summers I directed the nature center at a Christian camp in the Northwoods of Wisconsin, I often had paid help who assisted with teaching classes and operating the ministry. Before we embarked on the summer, I sat down with my assistants and explained to them that I was not their boss. The program director was not their boss. The executive director of the camp was not their boss. Jesus was their boss. I would be their mentor and leader, but they were to work and serve Him, not me. As our nature center was to focus on Jesus, it needed to be pure and holy. The buildings and aquariums needed to be cleaned and maintained, and the classes needed to be prepared. I tried to instill in them a good work ethic, offer teaching tips, and conduct Bible lessons. However, I also stressed the need to be fed daily through praying and studying the Word of God individually.

I was extremely blessed over the years there by these dozens of servants. Many of them really stand out in my mind. For instance, I remember coming into the nature center early in the morning and seeing some of them sitting at a table drinking tea and reading their Bibles together. Other times I came in and they were busy vacuuming the floor or cleaning an aquarium before going off to eat breakfast and then to the Bible sessions. I can recall walking back into the nature center after teaching an outdoor class to find them prepping for classes one or two days ahead. These people had an excellent balance of serving God and still listening to Him. At the end of each day we would sit, have a cup of tea or hot chocolate, discuss how the day went, and address the needs for the following day. We often bonded, and I still consider some of them as my adopted children. They would come over to my house to laugh and relax while eating the treats my wife made for them. They served God very well and at the same time, they grew closer to God. They found the balance.

Fan the Flame

Do you try to take control when you think someone is wrong? Have you ever been reprimanded for doing so? Explain.

Has anyone pointed out something about you that they think needs to change? What was it?

Have you tried to correct it, or do you ignore the advice thinking you are right in your actions or speech?

How would things change if you did take someone's advice?

Martha loved Christ Jesus and was learning more and more from him. Do you live a balanced life, one that includes "sitting at Jesus' feet"? If not, how can you adjust your schedule to make it more balanced?

Sitting at Jesus' feet involves a time of reading the Bible and talking with God about it. If you aren't reading His Word now, select one book in the Bible to concentrate on in small sections. The internet has free Bible websites you can use as well as a number of reading plans should you need them.

Final Thoughts

A college student and I sat down for tea late one afternoon to discuss some questions she had. She said, "I became a Christian in high school and my life really changed. I was on fire for God and was walking close with Him. But as I began college, I have noticed over these last few years that my walk has dwindled. I don't feel very close to Him right now. I want to walk close with Him, but it does not seem to work for me. What's wrong with me?" I could tell she was disturbed by this and that she was very serious. She sought me out to ask this question and to find answers.

Sitting back in my chair, I looked into her eyes and gently asked her if I could ask her a couple of questions. She nodded while sipping her tea. First, I asked if she was sure she was a Christian. She replied that she was very sure of that. She then reminded me of her salvation experience which was very sound. I had no reason to doubt her. Second, I asked her if there was some unconfessed and unrepentant sin that was setting up a roadblock in her life. She paused thoughtfully before answering that although she still sinned, she confessed and repented of it. I responded with affirmation. I asked her if she often talked with God. She inquired if I meant prayer and I nodded in the affirmative. She replied that she prayed daily but only at mealtimes. Then I asked her about her listening to God. I could tell from her expression that she was a bit puzzled by this. She asked if I meant reading her Bible. I nodded. She again paused for a long moment looking into her teacup and then she said quietly, "Michael, I haven't opened my Bible in eight months on my own. When I go to church I open it for the sermon, but that is all. Do you think that could be the trouble?"

I said to her in a gentle and loving way, "We have been friends for many years. One way that we have stayed close even when you live hundreds of miles away is that we talk often. The lines of communication are open, and we dialog. To keep a relationship close, you have to talk with your friend. You've stopped listening and talking with God which has damaged your relationship. You can't grow spiritually to your potential without listening to what God tells you in the 66 love letters He gave you."

Her smile indicated to me that she understood. She asked if she should get a yearly Bible to read. I told her instead to read short passages, looking for the who, what, when, where, why, and how in those verses. I added that she could begin by studying different biblical characters and examining what God could teach her through their lives.

That's how I got the idea to write this book and do this series. The conversation with this young lady made me think about how people often dismiss minor characters found in the Bible, missing the major lessons that they can teach us on keeping our walk with God alive and on fire. My hope and prayer are that you have found in these lessons keys on how to keep your fire burning for Jesus.

About Michael Lane

Michael hails from the South-side of Chicago and graduated from Olivet Nazarene University in 1979. He moved to the Bahamas where he met Denise, another teacher at the private Christian school he was employed at. They have three children and nine grandchildren. Michael did his graduate work at Northern Illinois University in biology and Southern Illinois University in molecular biology, where he also worked in fisheries genetics as a research assistant. He has taught both in public and private schools for 25 years and has received numerous prestigious state and national teaching awards. Michael has also worked at the John G. Shedd Aquarium in Chicago as an instructor of marine biology and as a curriculum writer. In 1999 Michael joined Fort Wilderness Ministries to develop the Nature Center program and serve as the Director of Education and as a Bible and Apologetics Teacher. There he developed many popular programs and lessons that he is known for today such as the Marine Biology Adventure and the Israel Trip which combine science, history and biblical evidence in hands-on experiences easy for anyone to learn and understand. In 2021, Michael founded the apologetics-focused ministry *Evidence 4 Faith* to continue equipping Christians across the country with the knowledge and tools to grow and defend the faith. Michael has published several books alongside developing online videos and podcasts on topics about the Bible, Biblical Archaelogy, and Science.

Michael with his wife, Denise.

About E4F

Evidence 4 Faith (E4F) is a 501(c)3 Christian apologetics minis-try based in Wisconsin. Founded in 2021, our mission is to move people from a state of unbelief and shallow convictions to a state of belief and deep faith in the living God through studying the evidence found in History, Science, the Bible, and Logic. We are building a free online library of apologetics courses, bringing free and low-cost workshops to communities, and organizing budget-friendly trips to connect your faith to the real world.

You can learn more about us and support our mission at *evidence4faith.org.*